Cocoa and Objective-C Cookbook

Move beyond basic Cocoa development using over 70 simple and effective recipes for Mac OS X development

Jeff Hawkins

PUBLISHING

BIRMINGHAM - MUMBAI

Cocoa and Objective-C Cookbook

First published: May 2011

Production Reference: 1180511

Published by Packt Publishing Ltd.
32 Lincoln Road
Olton
Birmingham, B27 6PA, UK.

ISBN 978-1-849690-38-6

www.packtpub.com

Cover Image by Asher Wishkerman (a.wishkerman@mpic.de)

Credits

Author

Jeff Hawkins

Reviewers

Hendrik Bruinsma

Jofell Gallardo

Piotr Isajew

Mario Mosca

Jorge Rodriguez

Acquisition Editor

Steven Wilding

Development Editor

Roger D'souza

Technical Editor

Dayan Hyames

Project Coordinator

Leena Purkait

Proofreader

Lesley Harrison

Indexer

Monica Ajmera Mehta

Production Coordinator

Shantanu Zagade

Cover Work

Shantanu Zagade

About the Author

Jeff Hawkins has been developing software solutions and applications for 19 years. He has worked for Adobe Systems supporting third party developers writing plug-ins for FrameMaker on the Macintosh, Windows, and Solaris platforms. He has also worked for a startup delivering prime time television shows via satellite to television stations across the United States. Jeff currently works in the Tools and Architecture group for ADP Inc. designing and coding solutions for enterprise payroll systems. Jeff has extensive experience working with C, C++, Objective-C, Java, and JavaScript. In his spare time, Jeff enjoys working with Apple's iOS developing mobile applications and games. Jeff is also a private pilot with a seaplane rating and has built and flown his own Van's RV-8 airplane.

I would like to thank my wife Sue for all the love and support while I worked on this project. Her understanding and patience while I shifted priorities was truly extraordinary.

I would like to thank Leena Purkait, Steven Wilding, Roger D'souza, and Mary Nadar and all the others at Packt Publishing who have made this book possible.

About the Reviewers

Hendrik Bruinsma is a Mobile Technology specialist at the Sogeti-group with a certification in Computer Sciences and Information Technology. He is currently working on several mobile projects for different architectures with changing international teams. With a background in embedded systems, Hendrik keeps a good eye on the limitations of mobile platforms and the requirements of his customers.

He has been working for Sogeti for almost five years in different roles. He is a solution-minded, innovative, and creative professional, always keen to learn about and apply the latest developments in his area of expertise. He is a passionate Apple fanboy.

Jofell Gallardo is a former developer for Insync Mac Edition (`Insynchq.com`). He is a technical consultant for iPad Interactive eBooks for Vibal Foundation's Ibong Adarna, Monkey and the Turtle, and Noli Me Tangere (`VibalFoundation.org`). He is an iOS software engineer for CrowdSauce (`CrowdSauce.com`)

All my hard work is for you guys, Mommy, Daddy, and my unrelenting brothers and sisters. Brendan and Slade, thank you for the opportunity. Sir Gus and Miss Tin for all the patience and trust. Terence for the greatest break of my life. Joseph Ross for the constant advice. The Vibal Foundation Tech Team for all the unforgettable happy moments building apps. And Leena, for finding me in this tech haystack.

Piotr Isajew has over 15 years of experience in software development, primarily for UNIX-like operating systems. During this period, he was managing a number of development teams, while working as an IT Manager and an IT Director for media and mobile marketing companies in Poland.

Currently he is involved in founding a start-up mobile messaging project, and teaches Objective-C programming in a private academy in Warsaw, Poland.

Mario Mosca is the CEO and founder of WakeApp S.r.l. , Apple development with over 10 years of experience. Mario has spent a large portion of his career on developing for MacOS, but also has a extensive background in training and development for other languages.

WakeApp was born from the desire for innovation of two IT professionals, to create something different from the lethargy of traditional consulting. Our goal is to create solutions that combine a pleasant viewing experience with an indispensable ease of use, looking for innovative ideas, presented to the public through the new digital delivery channels.

www.PacktPub.com

Support files, eBooks, discount offers and more

You might want to visit www.PacktPub.com for support files and downloads related to your book.

Did you know that Packt offers eBook versions of every book published, with PDF and ePub files available? You can upgrade to the eBook version at www.PacktPub.com and, as a print book customer, you are entitled to a discount on the eBook copy. Get in touch with us at service@packtpub.com for more details.

At www.PacktPub.com, you can also read a collection of free technical articles, sign up for a range of free newsletters, and receive exclusive discounts and offers on Packt books and eBooks.

http://PacktLib.PacktPub.com

Do you need instant solutions to your IT questions? PacktLib is Packt's online digital book library. Here, you can access, read, and search across Packt's entire library of books.

Why subscribe?

- ▶ Fully searchable across every book published by Packt
- ▶ Copy and paste, print, and bookmark content
- ▶ On demand and accessible via web browser

Free access for Packt account holders

If you have an account with Packt at www.PacktPub.com, you can use this to access PacktLib today and view nine entirely free books. Simply use your login credentials for immediate access.

This book is dedicated to Sue, Katherine, and Kelly.

Table of Contents

Preface

This book will guide you through many different areas of Cocoa using easy to follow recipes. These recipes will take you through the basics of Cocoa, such as using alerts, all the way to advanced topics like layered animations and Core Image filters. By working through the recipes in this book, you will be ready to build incredible Cocoa applications.

What this book covers

Chapter 1, User Interface Components covers the use of the basic interface components such as NSTable, NSOutlineView, and WebView.

Chapter 2, Custom Views explains how to create and use your own views.

Chapter 3, Handling Events introduces keyboard, mouse, and gesture events and interpreting these events in your applications.

Chapter 4, Using Animation explains how to put CALayers into motion.

Chapter 5, Objective-C 2.0 introduces the new LLVM compiler and enabling garbage collection.

Chapter 6, Application Architecture covers the most common patterns used in application design and development.

Chapter 7, Better Debugging covers tips for better debugging.

Chapter 8, System Integration explains how to add badges and menus to your applications Dock icon.

Chapter 9, Working with Files introduces archiving data and parsing of popular data formats.

Chapter 10, Working with the Web explains connecting your application to the web and working with proper data encodings.

Chapter 11, Working with Databases covers the integration of MySQL and SQLite databases into your applications.

Chapter 12, Multimedia introduces the addition of QuickTime movies and sound in your applications.

What you need for this book

Software	Download URL
Xcode 2.4	`http://developer.apple.com/`
Mac OS X 10.6 (Snow Leopard)	`http://apple.com`
MySQL	`http://dev.mysql.com/downloads/mysql/5.1.html`
Sparkle	`http://sparkle.andymatuschak.org/`
TouchJSON	`https://github.com/TouchCode/TouchJSON`

Who this book is for

This book is perfect for the Mac OS X Cocoa developer who is ready to move beyond the basics and dive into more advanced Cocoa topics.

Conventions

In this book, you will find a number of styles of text that distinguish between different kinds of information. Here are some examples of these styles, and an explanation of their meaning.

Code words in text are shown as follows: "Finally, we allocate and initialize our custom view by setting its location and size in the `applicationDidFinishLaunching:` method of the `CustomViewAppDelegate` class."

A block of code is set as follows:

```
NSImage *image = [NSImage imageNamed:@"LearningJQuery.jpg"];
[imageView setImage:image];
[imageView setImageScaling:NSImageScaleAxesIndependently];
[imageView setImageAlignment:NSImageAlignCenter];
```

Any command-line input or output is written as follows:

```
hawk:~ jhawkins$ mysql -u root -p
Enter password:
mysql> use cocoa
Database changed
mysql> select * from publishers;
```

New terms and **important words** are shown in bold. Words that you see on the screen, in menus or dialog boxes for example, appear in the text like this: "We can do this by right-clicking on one of the folders in the project and choosing **Add** and then choosing **Existing Files...**".

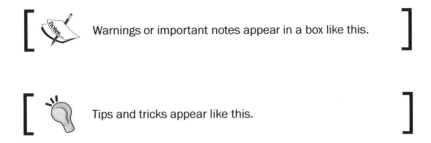

Warnings or important notes appear in a box like this.

Tips and tricks appear like this.

Reader feedback

Feedback from our readers is always welcome. Let us know what you think about this book—what you liked or may have disliked. Reader feedback is important for us to develop titles that you really get the most out of.

To send us general feedback, simply send an e-mail to feedback@packtpub.com, and mention the book title via the subject of your message.

If there is a book that you need and would like to see us publish, please send us a note in the **SUGGEST A TITLE** form on www.packtpub.com or e-mail suggest@packtpub.com.

If there is a topic that you have expertise in and you are interested in either writing or contributing to a book, see our author guide on www.packtpub.com/authors.

Customer support

Now that you are the proud owner of a Packt book, we have a number of things to help you to get the most from your purchase.

Downloading the example code

You can download the example code files for all Packt books you have purchased from your account at http://www.PacktPub.com. If you purchased this book elsewhere, you can visit http://www.PacktPub.com/support and register to have the files e-mailed directly to you.

Errata

Although we have taken every care to ensure the accuracy of our content, mistakes do happen. If you find a mistake in one of our books—maybe a mistake in the text or the code—we would be grateful if you would report this to us. By doing so, you can save other readers from frustration and help us improve subsequent versions of this book. If you find any errata, please report them by visiting `http://www.packtpub.com/support`, selecting your book, clicking on the **errata submission form** link, and entering the details of your errata. Once your errata are verified, your submission will be accepted and the errata will be uploaded on our website, or added to any list of existing errata, under the Errata section of that title. Any existing errata can be viewed by selecting your title from `http://www.packtpub.com/support`.

Piracy

Piracy of copyright material on the Internet is an ongoing problem across all media. At Packt, we take the protection of our copyright and licenses very seriously. If you come across any illegal copies of our works, in any form, on the Internet, please provide us with the location address or website name immediately so that we can pursue a remedy.

Please contact us at `copyright@packtpub.com` with a link to the suspected pirated material.

We appreciate your help in protecting our authors, and our ability to bring you valuable content.

Questions

You can contact us at `questions@packtpub.com` if you are having a problem with any aspect of the book, and we will do our best to address it.

1
User Interface Components

In this chapter, we will cover:

- ▶ Using a NSTableView
- ▶ Using a NSOutlineView
- ▶ Using NSSplitView
- ▶ Using the WebView
- ▶ Displaying a NSAlert
- ▶ Formatting dates
- ▶ Formatting numbers
- ▶ Importing images
- ▶ Saving preferences with NSUserDefaults
- ▶ Retrieving preferences with NSUserDefaults
- ▶ Adding a password to KeyChain
- ▶ Retrieving a password from KeyChain
- ▶ Accessing the Address Book
- ▶ Adding an event to iCal

Introduction

When building applications in Cocoa, there are several user interface components and concepts that are key to all applications. In this chapter, we will cover some of Cocoas more advanced and most often used interface elements. The formatting of dates and numbers will also be covered. How to best use alerts and sheets when you need to display errors or warnings to the user will also be covered. We will look at how to quickly save defaults or user preferences for your application. We will also work with KeyChain to illustrate how to securely store and retrieve passwords. Lastly, we will cover working with the address book and calendar stores.

Some recipes in this chapter require Mac OS X 10.6.

Using a NSTableView

The `NSTableView` is one of the most used Cocoa UI elements in Mac OS X. It is used everywhere from simple lists to complex interactive tables.

In this recipe, we will create a simple table view that will provide you with the basic information needed to implement and extend a table view in your application.

Getting ready

Start Xcode and choose **New Project...** from the **File** menu. Once the **New Project** dialog appears, choose the following options. Under **Mac OS X** in the left pane, select **Application**, then choose **Cocoa Application** and click on the **Choose...** button. Name your project **TableView** and save it:

How to do it...

1. Click on the `TableViewAppDelegate.h` file to open it so that we can modify the interface of the `TableViewAppDelegate` class.

2. First, lets add the `NSTableViewDataSource` protocol to the interface. This marks our class as implementing the methods required to be a data source for the table view:

```
@interface TableViewAppDelegate : NSObject <NSApplicationDelegate,
NSTableViewDataSource>
```

Downloading the example code

You can download the example code files for all Packt books you have purchased from your account at http://www.PacktPub.com. If you purchased this book elsewhere, you can visit http://www.PacktPub.com/support and register to have the files e-mailed directly to you.

1. We need to add two variables to the interface directly below the `NSWindow` reference. The first is a `NSTableView *tableView;` and the second is `NSMutableArray *tableData;` The `tableView` is a reference to the `NSTableView` we are going to add via Interface Builder and the second will act as a data source and will hold the sample data for our table view. We need to add a property for the `NSTableView` and we need to use the special keyword `IBOutlet` which allows Interface Builder to see our reference:

```
@property (assign) IBOutlet NSWindow *window;
@property (retain) IBOutlet NSTableView *tableView;
```

2. From the project view in Xcode, click on the `TableViewAppDelegate.m` so we can modify the implementation of our class.

3. We need to synthesize our `tableView` variable, so below the synthesized window variable, add `@synthesize tableView;`.

4. Next we need to implement some sample data for our table view. We will do that with the `tableData` variable that we added earlier. In the `applicationDidFinishLaunching:` method of our class, we will add three rows of data:

```
tableData = [[NSMutableArray alloc] init];

    // Row 1
    NSMutableDictionary *dictionary = [NSMutableDictionary
dictionary];
    [dictionary setObject:@"Benjamin Franklin" forKey:@"name"];
    [dictionary setObject:@"1/17/1706" forKey:@"birthdate"];
    [tableData addObject:dictionary];
```

```
// Row 2
dictionary = [NSMutableDictionary dictionary];
[dictionary setObject:@"Samuel Adams" forKey:@"name"];
[dictionary setObject:@"9/27/1722" forKey:@"birthdate"];
[tableData addObject:dictionary];

// Row 3
dictionary = [NSMutableDictionary dictionary];
[dictionary setObject:@"Thomas Jefferson" forKey:@"name"];
[dictionary setObject:@"4/13/1743" forKey:@"birthdate"];
[tableData addObject:dictionary];

[tableView reloadData];
```

5. There are two methods that we are required to implement as a data source for a table view. The first of those methods is `numberOfRowsInTableView:` which will tell the table view how many rows of data we need to display. The second method we need to implement is `tableView:objectValueForTableColumn:row:` This method will provide the data for the table view. We will pull our data from our data source based on the parameters passed to us in this method:

```
- (NSInteger) numberOfRowsInTableView:(NSTableView *)table {
    return [tableData count];
}

- (id)tableView:(NSTableView *)table
    objectValueForTableColumn:(NSTableColumn *)column
    row:(NSInteger)rowIndex {
  NSDictionary *rowData = [tableData objectAtIndex:rowIndex];

    return [rowData valueForKey:[column identifier]];
}
```

6. We are now ready to work with Interface Builder to lay out the table view. Double-click on the `MainMenu.xib` in Xcode's project view. This will open the user interface file in Interface Builder.

7. If the Library palette is not currently displayed in Interface Builder, choose **Library** from the **Tools** menu.

8. Drag a Table View from the Library to your window. You may want to adjust the table view to fully fill the window and automatically resize when the window resizes. This can be done from the **Sizes** tab of the Inspector. If the Inspector is not currently shown, you can display it from the **Tools** menu of Interface Builder.

9. Now we need to add some columns to our table view. Make sure you have selected the `NSTableView`, and then add a Name column and a Birth Date column to the table view. In order to do this, select the Inspector's **Attributes** tab and change the number of columns to two. By double-clicking on the first column, you can change the column's properties in the Inspector. Change the Title to **Name** and the identifier to **name**. Make the same changes to the second column. Its title should be **Birth Date** and its identifier should be **birthdate**.

10. In Interface Builder, we need to connect the table view to our references in the implementation of our class. In the main window of Interface Builder control, click on `Table View App Delegate`. The Outlets window will appear. Mouse over the hollow circle of the `tableView` Outlet, it should change to a plus inside the circle. Click and drag from the circle with the plus to the table view you dragged into the window earlier. You will see the Table View flash as an indicator that you have selected it. Release the mouse button and the connection will be complete:

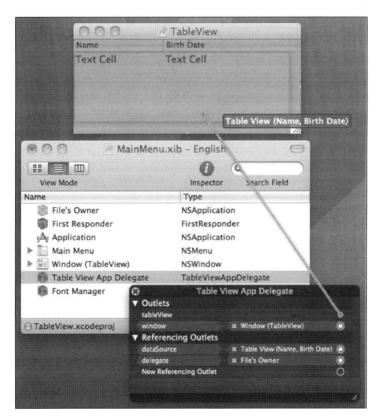

11. We now need to tell the table view that our `Table View App Delegate` will be the data source for the table view. Control click on the table view in your layout. From the Outlets window, mouse over the hollow circle for data source outlet. Click and drag over to the `Table View App Delegate` in the main window. When the `Table View App Delegate` highlights, release the mouse button:

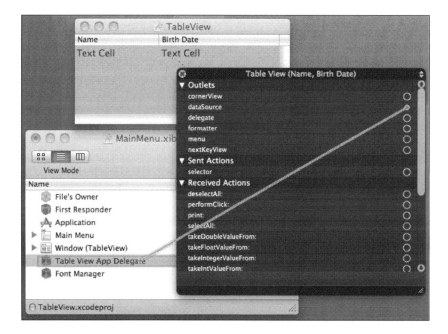

12. Back in Xcode, choose **Build and Run** to see the table view in action.

How it works...

Cocoa relies heavily on the delegation design pattern. Basically, your controller classes will act as the delegates for the Cocoa UI objects. In this example, our `TableViewAppDelegate` class is the delegate for the `NSTableView`. As the `NSTableView` goes through its redrawing process, it calls our class for the information it needs to draw the table, such as the number of rows and the data for each row and column. In our example, we used the `NSMutableArray` as a data source for the table view. The array contained `NSDictionaries` for each row, using a name and birth date for each column in the table view. You are not limited to using `NSArray`s for the data source. You may design your own custom class or data structure to contain your table view's data. In fact, most real world applications data is retrieved from a database or a file.

Next, we used Interface Builder to add the `NSTableView` to our application window. Interface Builder makes it easy to position UI elements and set their properties, something we would otherwise have to do via code. We also used Interface Builder to connect our `NSTableView` to its data source.

One last detail about the table view is the `reloadData` method. You will need to call this method when you change data in your data source. This will force the table view to redraw and in that process call your delegate methods and therefore update the table view with the latest changes in your data source.

There's more...

There are many other delegate methods that we can implement for the table view to handle such things as data being dropped on the table from a drag-and-drop operation or sorting the data in the table.

We can also provide the `NSTableView` with a custom view to fill the area where the horizontal and vertical scroll bars meet in the lower right-hand corner of the table view. This area is known as the corner view. By right-clicking on the table view within Interface Builder, we can assign our custom view.

Depending on your application design, it may be necessary to use a custom drawn cell in your table view. Cocoa makes this possible by allowing you to provide your own subclass of `NSCell`. To implement this you need to set your custom `NSCell` class on the table's column. You then implement the delegate method `willDisplayCell:` in your delegate's class. When the table view calls you during its drawing process, the cell parameter of `willDisplayCell:` will be an instance of your custom `NSCell` subclass. You can then set whatever custom properties your cell requires to draw itself.

See also

The sample code and project for this recipe is located under the `TableView` folder in the code bundled with this book.

Using a NSOutlineView

NSOutlineView's are the preferred method for displaying data in a hierarchal manner. In this recipe, we will create a simple outline view and describe the delegate methods you will need to implement in your controller class in order to display your data correctly.

Getting ready

In Xcode, choose **New Project**... from the **File** menu. As we have done in other recipes, choose **Application** from under the **Mac OS X** section and then choose **Cocoa Application**. Name the new project OutlineView and save.

How to do it...

1. Open the OutlineViewAppDelegate.h so that we can add the protocol, variables, and a property to our class interface.

2. Add the NSOutlineViewDelegate protocol to the class interface.

3. Next, we need to add our outline view variable reference. Below the NSWindow reference, add the following: NSOutlineView *outlineView;. We also need to add our data source variable: NSMutableDictionary *outlineViewData;.

4. We need to add a property for the outline view, so add: @property (retain) IBOutlet NSOutlineView *outlineView; below the property for the NSWindow.

5. Now, click on OutlineViewAppDelegate.m from the project view to open it.

6. Add @synthesize outlineView; below the line for the synthesized window.

7. We are now ready to work with Interface Builder to add the NSOutlineView to our applications window. Double-click on the MainMenu.xib in Xcode's project view. This will start Interface Builder and open our interface file.

8. Drag a Outline View from the Library to your window. You may want to adjust the outline view to fully fill the window and automatically resize when the window resizes.

9. Next, we need to connect the references, called outlets, in our code with the UI elements in Interface Builder. Control click on the `Outline View App Delegate` in the main window of Interface Builder. When the outlet's window appears, you will need to connect the outlineView outlet to the `NSOutlineView` that you dragged into the main window. Note that the `NSOutlineView` will flash when you have selected the outline view:

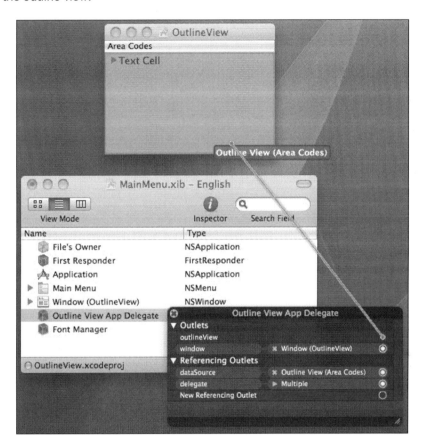

10. Control-click on the outline view you dragged into the window. Make a connection from the data source in the outlet window to the `Outline View App Delegate` in the main window:

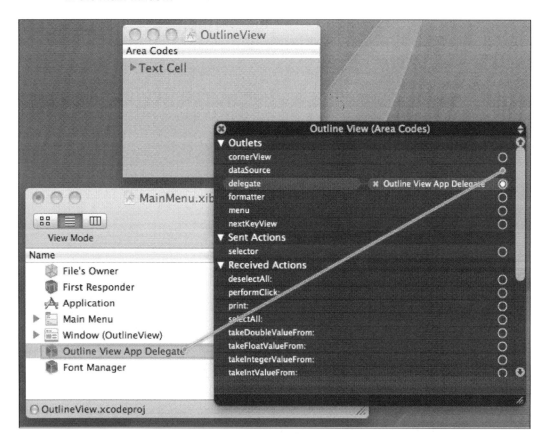

11. We now need to add some sample data for our data source. Note that we are going to use an `NSMutableDictionary` as our data source and this will contain all the root items for the outline view. Each of the items under the root item will be an `NSArray` of items. In this sample, it will be the U.S. Area Codes for its parent state.

12. Back in Xcode, we need to create some sample data for our outline view. In the `applicationDidFinishLaunching:` method lets add the following:

```
outlineViewData = [[NSMutableDictionary dictionary] retain];

// Item 1
NSArray *items = [NSArray arrayWithObjects:@"229", @"404", @"478",
  @"678", @"706", @"770", @"912", nil];
[outlineViewData setObject:items forKey:@"Georgia"];
```

```
// Item 2
items = [NSArray arrayWithObjects:@"240", @"301", @"410", @"443",
  nil];
[outlineViewData setObject:items forKey:@"Maryland"];

// Item 3
items = [NSArray arrayWithObjects:@"206", @"253", @"360", @"425",
  @"509", nil];
[outlineViewData setObject:items forKey:@"Washington"];

[outlineView reloadData];
```

13. Next, lets add the delegate methods that the outline view will call to populate the view. First, we need to implement `outlineView:numberOfChildrenOfItem:`. In this method, we need to return the number of child items for the passed item parameter. Note that if item is nil, we need to return the number of root items. In our example, this would be the number of entries in the `outlineViewData` dictionary. Since we are using `NSArray`'s and `NSDictionaries` in our data source implementation, we can simply return the count of items since both array's and dictionaries implement the count method:

```
- (NSInteger)outlineView:(NSOutlineView *)outlineView
    numberOfChildrenOfItem:(id)item {
  if (item == nil) {
    return [outlineViewData count];
  }

  return [item count];
}
```

14. The outline view needs to know which item from the data source to display for a particular index. We provide this information to the outline view by implementing the `outlineView:child:ofItem:` method. Since we are using arrays and dictionaries to hold data for the outline view, we use `isKindOfClass:` to determine if item is an array or dictionary. We can then determine how best to get to the data we need to return.

15. The next method our delegate needs to implement is `outlineView:objectValueForTableColumn:byItem:`. In this method, there are two types of objects that can represent the item parameter. Those types are `NSString` and `NSArray`. Note that these are the same types we use in our data source. Therefore, we need to use `isKindOfClass:` again to determine the type of item being passed to us. If the item is an `NSString`, we just return the item, otherwise we see if it is a array and if so, find the key in the `outlineViewData` dictionary that represents this array. We then return that key, or in our case the state's name.

16. The final delegate we will implement is the `outlineView:isItemExpandable:` method. We simply need to return whether or not the passed item is capable of being expanded. If the item is a dictionary or array that has an object count, then we return true.

17. Choose **Build and Run** from the toolbar in Xcode to test your outline view application.

How it works...

The outline view works by calling your delegate methods during the redrawing of the outline view. Some of the delegate methods that you implement will be called for each item in the outline view. This is important to remember since the type of the item parameter will be of the generic type `id` and you will have to determine what item really is using `isKindOfClass:` in order to return the correct information for the outline view.

Next, we used Interface Builder to add a `NSOutlineView` to our applications main window. Interface Builder also lets us set properties on the outline view to allow it to resize with the applications window at runtime.

We linked the outline view and data source references in our code with the outline view in Interface Builder so the `OutlineViewAppDelegate` class could act as the delegate and data source for the `NSOutlineView`.

As with the `NSTableView`, you can call the `reloadData` method to force a redraw of the outline view if the data in your data source changes.

There's more...

How you structure your data for the outline view's data source will make working with the outline view a bit easier. In our example, we used an `NSMutableDictionary` to hold all of the root items. We then used `NSArray`s to store all the items for each of the root items. This structure is simple, but may be added to if needed. We could add another `NSDictionary` in place of the `NSArray`'s and we would have another level in our hierarchy.

Since `NSOutlineView` is a subclass of `NSTableView`, you can think of the outline view as expanding and collapsing the table view's rows. The outline view also can have additional columns to display related information about its items. For example, if your outline view was showing a folder listing, you might have a column to show the folder's size in bytes or the number of items in the folder.

See also

The sample code and project for this recipe is located under the `OutlineView` folder in the code bundled with this book.

Using NSSplitView

A split view is a great way to have multiple resizable views within your application. A split view works well when you need to have a list of items in one area of the split view, commonly the top view, and a detail view in the other. Apple's `Mail.app` uses this approach to display items from your inbox in the top of the split view and then the actual message in the bottom view.

Getting ready

Let's head back into Xcode and create a new Project from the **File** menu. Lets save this project with the name `SplitView`.

How to do it...

1. As we have done in the other recipes in this chapter, we need to open the `SplitViewAppDelegate.h` to add the delegate, in this case a `NSSplitViewDelegate`, and a variable to the class interface. Below the reference to `NSWindow`, add the following variable `NSSplitView *splitView;`.

2. Next, we need to add a property for the split view variable. Below the property for the `NSWindow`, add: `@property (retain) IBOutlet NSSplitView *splitView;`.

3. Now its time to add a `NSSplitView` to our application's window using Interface Builder. In the project window of Xcode, double-click on the `MainMenu.xib` file to open the interface file.

4. From the Library palette in Interface Builder, locate the Horizontal Split View and drag it to the application window. You may want to adjust the split view's properties so that it is the same size as the window and resizes with the application window. This can be accomplished from the **Size** tab in the **Attributes Inspector**.

We now need to connect the split view to our reference in the code. Control click on the `Split View App Delegate` and from the outlets window, drag a connection from the `splitView` outlet to the split view in the applications window:

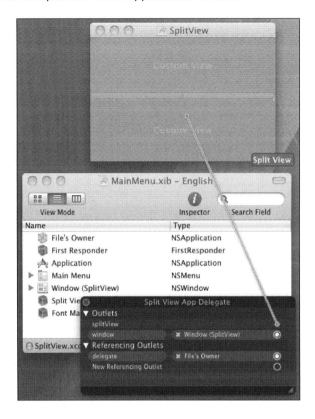

5. Back in Xcode, choose **Build and Run** from the toolbar. If all goes well, your application will run with a split view. Note that you can grab the divider and resize the split view.

How it works...

The split view is a pretty simple view in Cocoa and is really nothing more than a dynamic container for other Cocoa views or your own custom views.

There's more...

The NSSplitView class allows you to be notified via delegation when the user resizes the split view with the divider. As we have done in other recipes, you can use Interface Builder to connect the split view to your `Split View App Delegate`. After making this connection, you can implement one of the many delegate methods.

See also

The sample code and project for this recipe is located under the `SplitView` folder in the code bundled with this book.

Using the WebView

The `WebView` is used to embed web content in your application. Using a `WebView`, you can build advanced web browser functionality in your application.

Getting ready

In Xcode, lets create a new Cocoa Application project and save it as `WebView`.

How to do it...

1. The `WebView` is based on the WebKit framework, so we will need to include the `WebKit.framework` into our project. Right-click on `Frameworks` folder in the Project view of Xcode and choose **Add**, then choose **Existing Frameworks...** From the Frameworks window, choose **WebKit.framework**:

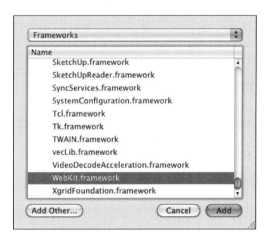

2. Open the `WebViewAppDelegate.h` file. We need to add the import for the `WebView` before we can use it. Below the `#import <Cocoa/Cocoa.h>`, add `#import <WebKit/WebKit.h>`

3. We also need to add a variable for our web view. Add `WebView *webView;` below the window variable.

4. Next, add a property for the webView variable: `@property (retain) IBOutlet WebView *webView;`

5. Open the `WebViewAppDelegate.m` file and add `@synthesize webView;` after `@synthesize` window.

6. Double-click on `MainMenu.xib` to open Interface Builder. Drag a Web View from the Library palette to the main window and adjust the size of the view to fit the window.

7. Next, we need to connect the outlet and delegate for the web view. Right-click on the `Web View App Delegate` and drag a connection from the webView outlet to the web view in the applications window. Next right-click on the web view in the applications window and drag a connection from `frameLoadDelegate` to the `Web View App Delegate`.

8. Next, lets add some code to display a web page in our web view. In the `applicationDidFinishLaunching:` method, let's add the following code:

    ```
    NSURL *url = [NSURL URLWithString:@"http://www.packtpub.com"];
    NSURLRequest *urlRequest = [NSURLRequest requestWithURL:url];
    [[webView mainFrame] loadRequest:urlRequest];
    ```

9. Click the **Build and Run** toolbar button in Xcode and let's see our web view in action.

How it works...

The WebView works by handling all the details of parsing and displaying HTML, CSS, and JavaScript for you. Basically, all you have to manage is the main frame and the URLs to the web content you want to display. Since Cocoa's `WebView` is based on WebKit, you can provide similar functionality to what is available in the Safari web browser included in Mac OS X.

There's more...

By implementing just a few of `WebView`'s delegate methods, our application can be notified when the title element has loaded and when the page has completed loading into the web view.

If you need to know the title element, implement the following delegate:

`webView:didReceiveTitle:forFrame:`. If you need to know when the page has finished loading, implement the `webView:didFinishLoadForFrame:` delegate method.

The sample code for this recipe has implemented both of these methods and displays an alert when we receive the notifications.

See also

The sample code and project for this recipe is located under the `WebView` folder in the code bundled with this book.

Displaying a NSAlert

At some point, while the user is interacting with your application, you will need to show them a message, warning, or even an error. The `NSAlert` class makes simple work of creating and displaying alerts. Cocoa provides simple methods for you to create alerts quickly and easily. Cocoa also provides two different ways to display modal dialogs. One is a dialog window and the other is a sheet that drops down from the parent window.

Getting ready

In Xcode, select the **File** menu and choose **New Project**... As we have done in the other recipes, we will create a new Cocoa Application. Name the project **Alert** and save. In this recipe, we are going to create a single button that will display several different types of alerts.

How to do it...

1. Open the `AlertAppDelegate.h` file and add a `NSButton` variable `*showAlertsButton` below the `NSWindow` variable.

2. Add a property for the button: `@property (retain) IBOutlet NSButton *showAlertsButton;`

3. Next, you will need to add a method signature for the button's action method. Add the `- (IBAction) showAlertsButtonHit:(id)sender;` signature to the class interface.

```
Open the AlertAppDelegate.m file so we can implement the
showAlertsButtonHit: action method:
- (void) showAlertsButtonHit:(id)sender {
  NSInteger result = NSRunAlertPanel(@"Title",
                    @"Message",
                    @"Default Button",
                    @"Alternate Button",
                    @"Other Button");

    result = NSRunCriticalAlertPanel(@"Title",
                @"Message",
                @"Default Button",
                @"Alternate Button",
                 @"Other Button");


    result = NSRunInformationalAlertPanel(@"Title",
                @"Message",
                @"Default Button",
```

```
                  @"Alternate Button",
                  @"Other Button");

   NSAlert *alert = [NSAlert alertWithMessageText:@"Alert Title"
            defaultButton:@"Default Button"
            alternateButton:@"Cancel"
            otherButton:@"Other Button"
            informativeTextWithFormat:@"Something bad has
               happened."];
   [alert runModal];


   alert = [NSAlert alertWithMessageText:@"Alert Title"
            defaultButton:@"Default Button"
            alternateButton:@"Cancel"
            otherButton:@"Other Button"
            informativeTextWithFormat:@"Something bad has
               happened."];

   [alert beginSheetModalForWindow:[self window]
            modalDelegate:self
            didEndSelector:@selector(sheetModalEnded:returnCode:
contextInfo:)
            contextInfo:nil];
}
```

4. Double-click on `MainMenu.xib` to open it in Interface Builder.

5. Drag a **Push Button** from the **Library** palette to the application window.

6. Connect the Push Button and the button's action method. Right-click on `Alert App Delegate` and drag a connection from the `showAlertsButton` outlet to the button in the main window.

7. Drag a connection from the `showAlertsButtonHit:` Received Action to the button in the main window.

8. Back in Xcode, choose **Build and Run** from the toolbar:

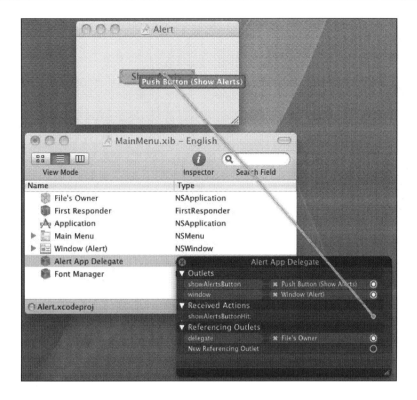

How it works...

Cocoa provides several C functions for quickly creating alerts. When using the C functions to create your alerts, you can determine which button the user has clicked by comparing the return value to one of the following constants: NSAlertDefaultReturn, NSAlertAlternateReturn, and NSAlertOtherReturn.

In the case of using a sheet, you must provide a delegate method that will be called when the alert is closed. This delegate method must have the following signature:

```
- (void) sheetModalEnded:(NSAlert *)alert returnCode:(NSInteger)retur
nCode contextInfo:(void *)contextInfo
```

Although the signature of the method must remain the same, the selector name, sheetModelEnded, can vary. This can be handy when using a single controller to handle many alerts.

The returnCode parameter will determine which button was used to close the alert. You should compare this value to the constants listed above.

There's more...

Using the `beginSheetModalForWindow:modalDelegate:didEndSelector:`
`contextInfo:` method for creating an alert is very flexible. You can display the alert in
one part of your application and handle the delegate to close the sheet in another part of
the application. You can use the `contextInfo:` parameter to pass an `NSDictionary` or
maybe an `NSArray` with values that you might need in determining the proper action to take
depending on which button the user clicked in the sheet.

See also

The sample code and project for this recipe is located under the `Alert` folder in the code
bundled with this book.

Formatting dates

When building applications, it is often necessary to work with dates. Cocoa provides the
`NSDateFormatter` class for working with dates. `NSDateFormatter` can convert dates to
strings and strings into dates. As we will see in this recipe, `NSDateFormatter` can also work
with relative dates such as "Today" and "Yesterday".

Getting ready

In this recipe, we will create a Cocoa application as we have done in other recipes.
However, we will be using `NSLog()` to display the results on the console rather than
the applications window.

In Xcode, let's create a new Cocoa Application project and save it as `DateFormat`.

How to do it...

In the following code sample, we have used all the possible styles to format the current date.
We have also used the `setDoesRelativeDateFormatting:YES` method so that we can
print relative dates.

Add the following code in the `applicationDidFinishLaunching:` method:

```
NSDateFormatter *formatter = [[[NSDateFormatter alloc] init]
    autorelease];

[formatter setTimeStyle:NSDateFormatterFullStyle];
[formatter setDateStyle:NSDateFormatterFullStyle];
NSLog(@"Full Style:    %@", [formatter stringFromDate:[NSDate
    date]]);
```

```
[formatter setTimeStyle:NSDateFormatterLongStyle];
[formatter setDateStyle:NSDateFormatterLongStyle];
NSLog(@"Long Style:   %@", [formatter stringFromDate:[NSDate
   date]]);

[formatter setTimeStyle:NSDateFormatterMediumStyle];
[formatter setDateStyle:NSDateFormatterMediumStyle];
NSLog(@"Medium Style: %@", [formatter stringFromDate:[NSDate
   date]]);

[formatter setTimeStyle:NSDateFormatterShortStyle];
[formatter setDateStyle:NSDateFormatterShortStyle];
NSLog(@"Short Style:  %@", [formatter stringFromDate:[NSDate
   date]]);

[formatter setTimeStyle:NSDateFormatterNoStyle];
[formatter setDateStyle:NSDateFormatterFullStyle];
NSLog(@"No Time:      %@", [formatter stringFromDate:[NSDate
   date]]);

[formatter setTimeStyle:NSDateFormatterFullStyle];
[formatter setDateStyle:NSDateFormatterNoStyle];
NSLog(@"No Date:      %@", [formatter stringFromDate:[NSDate
   date]]);

[formatter setTimeStyle:NSDateFormatterNoStyle];
[formatter setDateStyle:NSDateFormatterFullStyle];
[formatter setDoesRelativeDateFormatting:YES];
NSLog(@"Relative:     %@", [formatter stringFromDate:[NSDate
   date]]);

[formatter setDateStyle:NSDateFormatterShortStyle];
NSDate *date = [formatter dateFromString:@"9/10/2010"];
NSLog(@"Date String:  %@", [date description]);
```

How it works...

The `NSDateFormatter` formats the date and time depending on the style constants you set.
It's also possible to set no style for either date or time.

There's more...

When converting a string to a date, it is important to remember that the date string should be in the same format as the style you have set in the formatter. You will notice in the code example above that I have the time set to `NSDateFormatterNoStyle` and the date set to `NSDateFormatterShortStyle` and my date string is `"9/10/2010"`.

See also

The sample code and project for this recipe is located under the `DateFormat` folder in the code bundled with this book.

Formatting numbers

Applications often have to work with numbers that need to be displayed to the user as percentages or currency and so on. Using Cocoa, formatting numbers is quite easy, as this recipe will show.

Getting ready

Create a new Cocoa Application project and save it as `NumberFormat`. We will be adding our code to the `applicationDidFinishLaunching:` method of this applications delegate. As with the *Formatting dates* recipe, we will see our number formatting on the console rather than in the applications window.

How to do it...

In the sample code, we use the five different number format styles to format an `NSNumber` object. You can also provide `NSNumberFormatter` with a `NSLocale` which will help with localization of numbers. Note how we set a Spanish local when using the `NSNumberFormatterSpellOutStyle` style. This converts the spelled out number to Spanish.

Add the following code in the `applicationDidFinishLaunching:` method:

```
NSNumberFormatter *formatter = [[[NSNumberFormatter alloc] init]
    autorelease];

NSNumber *number = [NSNumber numberWithDouble:1234.99];
[formatter setNumberStyle:NSNumberFormatterDecimalStyle];
NSLog(@"Decimal Style: %@", [formatter stringFromNumber:number]);

number = [NSNumber numberWithDouble:.2];
```

```
[formatter setNumberStyle:NSNumberFormatterPercentStyle];
NSLog(@"Percent Style: %@", [formatter stringFromNumber:number]);

number = [NSNumber numberWithDouble:200.95];
[formatter setNumberStyle:NSNumberFormatterCurrencyStyle];
NSLog(@"Currency Style: %@", [formatter stringFromNumber:number]);

number = [NSNumber numberWithDouble:200.95];
[formatter setNumberStyle:NSNumberFormatterScientificStyle];
NSLog(@"Scientific Style: %@", [formatter
  stringFromNumber:number]);

number = [NSNumber numberWithDouble:200.95];
[formatter setNumberStyle:NSNumberFormatterSpellOutStyle];
NSLog(@"Spelled Out Style: %@", [formatter
  stringFromNumber:number]);

NSLocale *locale = [[[NSLocale alloc]
  initWithLocaleIdentifier:@"es"] autorelease];
[formatter setLocale:locale];
NSLog(@"Spelled Out Style: %@", [formatter
  stringFromNumber:number]);
```

How it works...

NSNumberFormater formats strings and numbers in a variety of formats. The number formatter will handle adding number separators, percent signs and currency symbols automatically, based on the locale.

There's more...

NSNumberFormatter also has methods to support rounding numbers if needed. This is done through the setRoundingMode: method.

See also

The sample code and project for this recipe is located under the NumberFormat folder in the code bundled with this book.

Importing images

Every Mac OS X application uses images within the user interface. Adding an image using `NSImage` is pretty straightforward as long as you use one of the support formats. The formats supported by `NSImage` are: JPEG, TIFF, GIF, PNG, PICT, BMP, ICNS, and ICO.

Getting ready

Lets create a new Cocoa Application project in Xcode and save it as `Image`.

How to do it...

1. Open `ImageAppDelegate.h` so we can add a `NSImageView *imageView` variable to the class interface. Be sure to add a property for the image view as well:

   ```
   @property (retain) IBOutlet NSImageView *imageView;
   ```

2. Next, we need to open `ImageAppDelegate.m` so that we can add the `@synthesize imageView;` below the synthesized window.

3. In the `applicationDidFinishLaunching:` method, lets add the following code:

   ```
   NSImage *image = [NSImage imageNamed:@"LearningJQuery.jpg"];
   [imageView setImage:image];
   [imageView setImageScaling:NSImageScaleAxesIndependently];
   [imageView setImageAlignment:NSImageAlignCenter];
   ```

4. We need to add the image that we want to import into our Xcode project. We can do this by right-clicking on one of the folders in the project and choosing **Add** and then choosing **Existing Files...**

5. Double-click on `MainMenu.xib` in Xcode's project view to open the interface file in Interface Builder.

6. In the **Library** palette, find the **Custom View** and drag it into the applications window.

7. Select the **Identity** tab in the **Inspector** palette and set the **Class** popup to `NSImageView`.

8. Right-click on the `Image View App Delegate` and drag a connection from imageView to the CustomView (note that the custom view is now labeled `NSImageView`) that you dragged into the application window:

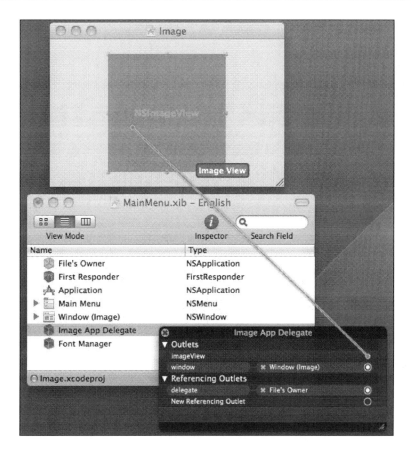

9. Head back to Xcode and choose **Build and Run** from the toolbar.

How it works...

The NSImage class' imageNamed: method will search the image cache, your applications main bundle, or the AppKit's bundle for the passed image name and if found, loads it from disk into the NSImage instance. We then call the setImage: method on the NSImageView to set the image instance. The NSImageView will draw the image within its view and possibly scale the image depending on the value set with the setImageScaling: method.

There's more...

You can set different options on how NSImageView will scale the image you provide based on whether your image is larger or smaller than the image view. You can also tell NSImageView not to scale at all.

See also

The sample code and project for this recipe is located under the `Image` folder in the code bundled with this book.

Saving preferences with NSUserDefaults

Many applications have preferences or other options that they need to save between application launches. Cocoa provides the `NSUserDefaults` class for this very task. As long as your preference is one of the standard C types or one of Cocoa's types, it can be used with `NSUserDefaults`. The following Cocoa types can be saved with `NSUserDefaults`: NSData, NSString, NSNumber, NSDate, NSArray, or NSDictionary. Note that the NSArray and NSDictionary can only contain instances of the previous four classes.

Getting ready

In Xcode, create a new Cocoa Application project and save it as `UserDefaults`.

How to do it...

Open the `UserDefaultsAppDelegate.m` file and add the following in the `applicationDidFinishLaunching:` method:

```
NSUserDefaults *defaults = [NSUserDefaults standardUserDefaults];

if ([defaults objectForKey:@"Publisher"]) {
  NSLog(@"Found: %@", [defaults objectForKey:@"Publisher"]);
} else {
  NSLog(@"Did not find Publisher.");
}


NSInteger count = [defaults integerForKey:@"Count"];
NSLog(@"Current Count: %d", count);
count++;

[defaults setInteger:count forKey:@"Count"];
[defaults setObject:@"Packt Publishing" forKey:@"Publisher"];
```

How it works...

The first time that you run this code, it will save two values to the preferences. The first is just a integer count; and the second is the publishers name. If you quit the application and run it again, the application will print "Found: Packt Publishing".

To save the values in the preference system, we use `setInteger:forKey:` and `setObject:forKey:` methods. The `setObject:forKey:` method can save any of the Cocoa types such as `NSString`, `NSArray`, `NSData` and `NSDictionary`.

There's more...

The standard C types may also be stored in the preference system using methods for the appropriate types such as `setInteger:forKey:` for integers, `setFloat:forKey:` for floats, and `setDecimal:forKey:` for decimals.

See also

The sample code and project for this recipe is located under the `UserDefaults` folder in the code bundled with this book.

Retrieving preferences with NSUserDefaults

In the previous recipe, *Saving preferences with NSUserDefaults*, we saved two values to the preferences system. In this recipe, we will retrieve those values.

Getting ready

Let's open the `UserDefaults` project that we used in the previous recipe.

How to do it...

In the `UserDefaultsAppDelegate.m` file, we have the following code. Add the following code to the `applicationDidFinishLaunching:` method:

```
NSUserDefaults *defaults = [NSUserDefaults standardUserDefaults];

if ([defaults objectForKey:@"Publisher"]) {
  NSLog(@"Found: %@", [defaults objectForKey:@"Publisher"]);
} else {
  NSLog(@"Did not find Publisher.");
}


NSInteger count = [defaults integerForKey:@"Count"];
NSLog(@"Current Count: %d", count);
count++;

[defaults setInteger:count forKey:@"Count"];
[defaults setObject:@"Packt Publishing" forKey:@"Publisher"];
```

How it works...

Running this code will return the count and the name of the publisher, "Packt Publishing". Each time you run the application, we add one to the count and save it back to the preferences.

We use the `integerForKey:` method to return the count and `objectForKey:` to return the publisher as a `NSString`.

Note that the values returned from the `objectForKey:` method are immutable, and therefore cannot be modified even if you are using one of the `NSMutable` variants when saving user defaults.

There's more...

You can examine all application preferences using the *defaults* command line utility. As an example, we can show hidden applications in the Dock by using the following command:

```
defaults write com.apple.Dock showhidden -bool YES
```

For more information on the defaults command, start the `Terminal.app` and type `man defaults`.

See also

The sample code and project for this recipe is located under the `UserDefaults` folder in the code bundled with this book.

Adding a password to KeyChain

The KeyChain application provides users with secure methods of storing passwords and certificates in Mac OS X. Cocoa applications can store passwords in KeyChain by using a single method provided by the KeyChain Services interface.

Getting ready

In Xcode, create a new Cocoa Application project and save it as `KeyChain`.

In order to use the KeyChain Services, we need to add the `Security.framework` to our Xcode project and add `#import <Security/Security.h>` to our classes header file.

How to do it...

To store the password in KeyChain, we call the `SecKeychainAddGenericPassword()` method. Since we are using the default key chain, we can pass NULL for the first parameter. We pass the name of the application for the service name. The account name and password are set. Since we don't need the key chain's item reference, we simply pass NULL for the last parameter.

Lastly, we check the return value to ensure that the password was set without error.

Add the following code to the `applicationDidFinishLaunching:` method:

```
status = SecKeychainAddGenericPassword(NULL,
                    [serviceName length],
                    [serviceName UTF8String],
                    [accountName length],
                    [accountName UTF8String],
                    [password length],
                    [password UTF8String],
                    NULL);
```

How it works...

The KeyChain Services provided by Cocoa provides a secure method of storing passwords and other protected data using the KeyChain programming interface.

There's more...

After running the sample application, you can start `KeyChain Access.app` and search for the account name to verify that your password was saved.

See also

The sample code and project for this recipe is located under the `KeyChain` folder in the code bundled with this book.

Retrieving a password from KeyChain

We have seen how to store a password using KeyChain Services in the previous recipe. Now lets retrieve the password that we stored in the previous recipe.

Getting ready

In this recipe, we will continue with the sample application that we created in the *Adding a password to KeyChain* recipe.

How to do it...

1. To retrieve the password from KeyChain, we call the
   `SecKeychainFindGenericPassword()` method. Since we are using the default key chain we pass NULL for the first parameter. Next, we need to use the same service name and account name that we used when storing the password. The next two parameters are both pointers. The first is the password length, a UInt32, which will be set to the length of the password on return. The second pointer is a void pointer for the password itself:

   ```
   status = SecKeychainFindGenericPassword (NULL,
                           [serviceName length],
                           [serviceName UTF8String],
                           [accountName length],
                           [accountName UTF8String],
                           &bufferLength,
                           &buffer,
                           NULL);
   ```

2. Note that you must free the void password pointer since the KeyChain Services interface has allocated the memory. You free the memory with a call to `SecKeychainItemFreeContent()` passing NULL for the first parameter and the buffer to free in the second parameter:

   ```
   SecKeychainItemFreeContent(NULL, buffer);
   ```

How it works...

The `SecKeychainFindGenericPassword()` method searches KeyChain for the password stored under the service name and account name. If the password is found, the return value will equal `errSecSuccess` and the password will be returned in the allocated buffer.

There's more...

When the `SecKeychainFindGenericPassword()` is called, KeyChain Services will alert the user asking for permission to access the KeyChain:

See also

The sample code and project for this recipe is located under the `KeyChain` folder in the code bundled with this book.

Accessing the Address Book

The Address Book is a system-wide database of contacts usually managed with the Address Book application. Cocoa applications have access to the contacts in the Address Book application through the `ABAddressBook` and the `ABPerson` interface.

Let's add a new organization to the address book and then list all the names and companies in our address book.

Getting ready

In Xcode, create a new Cocoa Application project and save it as `AddressBook`.

How to do it...

1. The first thing we need to add to our Xcode project is the AddressBook framework. Right-click on the `Frameworks` folder in the project view and choose **Add**, then choose **Existing Frameworks**. Find `AddressBook.framework` in the list of frameworks and click on **Add**.

2. Next, let's open the `AddressBookAppDelegate.h`. We need to add `#import <AddressBook/AddressBook.h>` below the existing import for Cocoa.

3. Now let's open the `AddressBookAppDelegate.m` and add the following code:

```
ABAddressBook *book = [ABAddressBook sharedAddressBook];

ABPerson *newPerson = [[[ABPerson alloc]      initWithAddressBook:
book]
   autorelease];
   [newPerson setValue:@"Packt Publishing" forProperty:
kABOrganizationProperty];
[book save];

NSArray *people  = [book people];

  for (ABPerson *person in people) {

    NSString *first = [person valueForProperty:
kABFirstNameProperty];
    NSString *last = [person valueForProperty:
kABLastNameProperty];
    NSString *company = [person
      valueForProperty:kABOrganizationProperty];

    if (first != nil && last != nil) {
      NSLog(@"Name: %@ %@", first, last);
    } else if (company != nil) {
      NSLog(@"Name: %@", company);
    }
  }
```

How it works...

First, we get a reference to the shared AddressBook, which in this case we will call "book". Next we allocate an `ABPerson` object for the new company that we are going to add to the address book. We set the value of the new persons `kABOrganizationProperty` to "Packt Publishing". Finally, we call the save method on the shared address book to save the new person in the contacts.

To get an array of all the people and organizations in the address book, we call the `people` method on the shared address book's reference. The array will be returned with `ABPerson` objects, which can then be queried for various properties such as the `kABFirstNameProperty` and `kABLastNameProperty`.

There's more...

The `ABPerson` class can be thought of as a type of dictionary. There are several keys that can be used with the `valueForProperty:` method to obtain information about a person. Some other properties supported by the `ABPerson` object are: `kABAddressProperty`, `kABEmailProperty`, and `kABBirthdayProperty`.

See also

The sample code and project for this recipe is located under the `AddressBook` folder in the code bundled with this book.

Adding an event to iCal

iCal is a single database Calendar Store from which you have access to all calendars, events, and tasks. You access these items in the Calendar Store via `CalCalendarStore` interface.

Getting ready

In Xcode, let's create a new Cocoa Application project and save it as `Calendars`.

How to do it...

1. This recipe assumes that you have a calendar called "Book" in iCal. To add the calendar, start the iCal application. Choose **File** and then choose **New Calendar....** When the new calendar is added, name it **Book**.

2. Right-click on the `Frameworks` folder in the project view of Xcode. Choose **Add** and then choose **Existing Frameworks**. Select the `CalendarStore.framework` and choose **Add**.

3. Next, lets open the `CalendarsAppDelegate.h` file and add `#import <CalendarStore/CalendarStore.h>` below the import for `Cooca.h`.

4. Open the `CalendarsAppDelegate.m` file and add the following code in the `applicationDidFinishLaunching:` method:

```
CalCalendarStore *calendarStore = [CalCalendarStore
   defaultCalendarStore];
NSArray *calendars = [calendarStore calendars];

   for (CalCalendar *calendar in calendars) {
      if ([[calendar title] isEqualToString:@"Book"] == YES) {
```

```
        NSDate *startDate =
            [NSDate dateWithString:@"2010-11-05 10:00:00 -0400"];
        NSDate *endDate = [NSDate dateWithString:@"2010-11-05
   11:00:00
            -0400"];

        CalEvent *event = [CalEvent event];
        [event setTitle:@"Chapter Review"];
        [event setLocation:@"Bill's Office"];
        [event setStartDate:startDate];
        [event setEndDate:endDate];
        [event setCalendar:calendar];

        NSError *error;
        [calendarStore saveEvent:event span:CalSpanThisEvent
            error:&error];

        break;
    }
}
```

How it works...

We first get a reference to the default calendar store. We then get an NSArray of all the calendars in the calendar store.

Next, we look at all the calendars in the calendar store for a calendar with a title of "Book". If we find the calendar, we create a new CalEvent instance with a title of "Chapter Review" and set a few other properties. We need to add a starting and ending date for the event, so we use NSDate's dateWithString: method to create both dates. To associate the event with the book calendar, we call the setCalendar: method. The last thing that we need to do is to save the event with the calendar store's saveEvent:span:error: method.

If you run this application and then open the iCal application, the new event will be shown in the Book calendar on the starting date that you set.

There's more...

Through the Cocoa notification mechanism, your application can receive notifications when other applications add, update, or delete calendars, events, or tasks to the calendar store. To receive these notifications you need to register for them with the NSNotificationCenter.

See also

The sample code and project for this recipe is located under the Calendars folder in the code bundled with this book.

2
Custom Views

In this chapter, we will cover:

- ▶ Drawing in your custom view
- ▶ Using your custom view in Interface Builder
- ▶ Handling mouse events in your view
- ▶ Handling keyboard events in your view
- ▶ Drawing strings with attributes

Introduction

A custom view provides a way to add polish and character to your application. Using a custom view or a combination of custom views, you can make your application's design stand out by presenting the display of data in a unique way.

During this chapter, we will continue to build on the custom view as we work through each of the recipes. The finished view will look similar to the one below. After learning how to draw our custom view, we will modify the view to handle mouse and keyboard events. We will also add a title to our view by drawing an attributed string in the title bar.

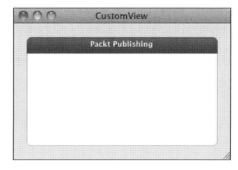

Drawing in your custom view

In this recipe, we will begin drawing our custom view using Cocoa's drawing classes. We will also load images and use them in our custom view to draw the title bar at the top of our view.

Getting ready

In Xcode, create a new Cocoa Application project and save it as `CustomView`.

How to do it...

1. In the Project view, right-click on **Classes** and choose **Add**, then choose **New File...** Under the **Mac OS X** section, select **Cocoa Class**. Click on the **Objective-C Class** icon. Be sure to choose `NSView` from the Subclass of popup. Name the new file `MyView.m`:

2. Double-click on the `MyView.m` file to open it and add the following code in the `drawR ect:(NSRect)dirtyRect` method of MyView's implementation:

```
NSImage *left = [NSImage imageNamed:@"left.png"];
NSImage *middle = [NSImage imageNamed:@"middle.png"];
NSImage *right = [NSImage imageNamed:@"right.png"];


NSBezierPath *path = [NSBezierPath bezierPathWithRoundedRect:[self
   bounds] xRadius:8.0 yRadius:8.0];
[path setClip];


[[NSColor whiteColor] setFill];
[NSBezierPath fillRect:[self bounds]];


[[NSColor grayColor] setStroke];
[path stroke];


NSPoint point = NSMakePoint(0, [self bounds].size.height - ([left
   size].height));
[left drawAtPoint:point fromRect:NSZeroRect
   operation:NSCompositeSourceOver fraction:1.0];


NSRect rect = NSMakeRect([left size].width,
                [self bounds].size.height - [middle size].height,
                [self bounds].size.width - ([left size].width -
[right
                   size].width),
                [middle size].height);
[middle drawInRect:rect fromRect:NSZeroRect
   operation:NSCompositeSourceOver fraction:1.0];


point = NSMakePoint([self bounds].size.width - ([right size].
width),
   [self bounds].size.height - ([right size].height));
[right drawAtPoint:point fromRect:NSZeroRect
   operation:NSCompositeSourceOver fraction:1.0];
```

3. We need to add the three images that we used to build the title bar into the Xcode project. For each of the images, right-click on **Classes** in the Xcode project. Choose **Add**... and then select **Existing Files...** Choose the image file you want to add to the project and click **Add**.

4. Double-click on `CustomViewAppDelegate.m` to open it.

5. Add the import for our custom view class:

```
#import "MyView.h"
```

6. Add the following code to the `applicationDidFinishLoading:` method:

```
NSRect frame = NSMakeRect(10.0, 10.0, 285.0, 160.0);
MyViewMyViewMyView *myView = [[MyView alloc] initWithFrame:frame];

[[[self window] contentView] addSubview:myView];
[myView release];
```

7. Back in Xcode, choose **Build and Run** from the toolbar to run the Custom View application.

How it works...

Drawing our custom view begins with drawing a rounded rectangle with a white fill and stroked in gray. Using the three images we loaded at the beginning of the `drawRect:` method, we draw the left, middle, and right images. Since Cocoa draws starting with the lower-left corner, we calculate the starting point and the size of the rectangles needed to draw the images by using the dimensions of our custom view and the dimensions of the images.

Finally, we allocate and initialize our custom view by setting its location and size in the `applicationDidFinishLaunching:` method of the `CustomViewAppDelegate` class. We then add it to the application window's content view.

There's more...

Because your view could be asked to draw itself often, you should allocate and retain resources, such as images, in the class's `initWithFrame:` or `awakeFromNib` methods, and then release them in the view's `dealloc:` method.

See also

The sample code and project for this recipe is located under the `CustomView` folder in the code bundled with this book.

Using your custom view in Interface Builder

In this recipe, we will be using Interface Builder to define the size and location of our custom view. In the last recipe *Drawing in your custom view*, we created our view programmatically by specifying the view's frame and then adding the view to the windows content view. Using Interface Builder to define your views makes it simpler to visually lay out your interface and set various properties, such as resizing.

Getting ready

Rather than creating a new Xcode project for this recipe, let's duplicate the project from the last recipe *Drawing in your custom view*.

How to do it...

1. Open the file `CustomViewAppDelegate.m` by double-clicking on it.

2. Remove or comment out all the code in the `applicationDidFinishLaunching:` method.

3. Double-click on the `MainMenu.xib` file to open it in Interface Builder. In Interface Builder's Library palette, locate the Custom View and drag it onto the applications window.

4. Select the **Size** tab from the Inspector pallet and adjust the **AutoSizing** so our view will resize with the applications window:

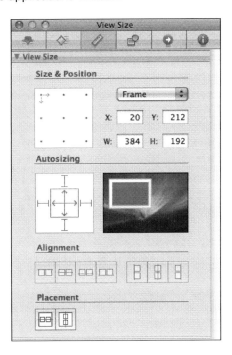

5. Click on the **Identity** tab in the Inspector's pallet and type or select **MyView** from the **Class** popup.

6. Choose **Save** from the **File** menu to save your changes:

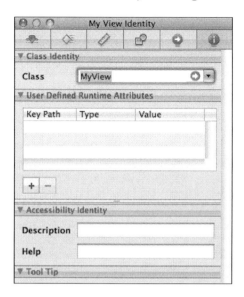

7. Back in Xcode, choose **Build and Run** to start the application. Note that when you resize the applications window, the custom view also resizes.

How it works...

Using Interface Builder, we assign our MyView class as the Class Identity to the custom view we dragged into the application window. Interface Builder stores the connection using the name of the class in the `MainMenu.xib` file the application loads at startup. While loading the `MainMenu.xib`, the MyView class is instantiated for you automatically and the MyView's `awakeFromNib` method is called. The `awakeFromNib` method is called to enable you to set any other properties that may be needed before the view is displayed. When `awakeFromNib` is called, the MyView view object has been loaded and initialized and all outlet connections have been made.

There's more...

When you use Interface Builder to layout your custom views, the `initWithFrame:` method of your view will still be called. However, when it is called, none of the outlet connections you have made in Interface Builder will be connected. This is why Cocoa provides the `awakeFromNib` method. When `awakeFromNib` is called on your view, the outlet connections and targets will have been made.

The sample code and project for this recipe is located under the `CustomView Interface Builder` folder in the code bundled with this book.

Handling mouse events in your view

In this recipe, we will add mouse event handling to the custom view we have been working on throughout this chapter. We will modify the MyView class to handle mouse down events and we will also add code to track the mouse moving in and out of our view. When you click on our view, it will display an alert and when you move the mouse in and out of the view, we will change the color of the view.

Getting ready

Rather than creating a new Xcode project for this recipe, lets duplicate the project from the last recipe *Using your custom view in Interface Builder*. You can duplicate the project using the Finders **Duplicate** command on the **File** menu.

How to do it...

1. Open the duplicate project that you just created in Xcode.

2. Double-click on the `MyView.h` class to open it.

3. Since our custom view will change fill colors when the mouse enters the view, we need to add a variable to hold the current fill color. Add the following variable to the MyView class interface:

   `NSColor *fillColor;`

4. We also need to add a variable for the tracking rectangle tag. Add the following after the `fillColor` variable:

   `NSTrackingRectTag trackingTag;`

5. Double-click on the `MyView.m` class file to open it.

6. In the `drawRect:` method, you will need to change the line where we fill the rectangle to use our `fillColor` variable. Change `[[NSColor whiteColor] setFill];` to `[fillColor setFill];`.

7. We need to override some methods from the `NSResponder` class to receive the mouse events we are interested in. Add the following new methods to the MyView class implementation:

```
- (void) mouseDown:(NSEvent *)theEvent {
  NSAlert *alert = [NSAlert alertWithMessageText:@"Received mouse
    down in MyView."
                      defaultButton:@"OK"
                      alternateButton:nil
                        otherButton:nil
              informativeTextWithFormat:@"Mouse Down"];
  [alert runModal];
}


- (void) mouseEntered:(NSEvent *)theEvent {
  fillColor = [NSColor grayColor];
  [self setNeedsDisplay:YES];
}


- (void) mouseExited:(NSEvent *)theEvent {
  fillColor = [NSColor whiteColor];
  [self setNeedsDisplay:YES];
}


- (void) updateTrackingAreas {

  [self removeTrackingRect:trackingTag];
  trackingTag = [self addTrackingRect:[self bounds] owner:self
    userData:nil assumeInside:NO];

  [super updateTrackingAreas];
}
```

8. Next, we need to add some code to track the mouse entering and exiting the view. We will call the `NSView` method `addTrackingRect:` to add our view's bounds rectangle. To do this, we will add the `awakeFromNib` method to our view. Also note that we set the `fillColor` variable to default to white:

```
- (void) awakeFromNib {
  trackingTag = [self addTrackingRect:[self bounds] owner:self
    userData:nil assumeInside:NO];
  fillColor = [NSColor whiteColor];
}
```

9. Choose **Build and Run** from the Xcode toolbar to run the application.

How it works...

Since our view is derived from `NSView`, which is derived from `NSResponder`, we only need to override the `mouseDown:` method in our `MyView` class to handle mouse down events in our view.

In order to handle the mouse entered and mouse exited events in the view, we need to add the bounds rectangle of our view as a tracking rectangle. We do this with the `addTrackingRect:` method and saving the returned tracking tag in our class variable. We save the tracking tag because we need it to update the tacking rectangle when the user resizes the view. When this happens, the `updateTrackingAreas:` method of our view is called. Here we remove the old rectangle and add the new one.

When the mouse enters the custom view, the `mouseEntered:` is called and when the mouse leaves the view, the `mouseExited:` is called. In these methods, we set the fill color and tell the view to redraw itself using the `[self setNeedsDisplay:YES]` method.

There's more...

If you need more control over when mouse events are sent to your view, you can use the `addTrackingArea:` method to add an `NSTrackingArea` with its options configured to your needs.

See also

The sample code and project for this recipe is located under the `MouseEvents` folder in the code bundled with this book.

Handling keyboard events in your view

In this recipe, we will modify the code we have been working with in this chapter to add keyboard handling to our view. Our view will be modified so when you type the following keys, the view will be filled with different colors:

Key	Color
r	Red
y	Yellow
b	Blue

Getting ready

Before adding keyboard events to our custom view, lets duplicate the Xcode project we used in the last recipe *Handling mouse events in your view*, and name it `KeyboardEvents`.

How to do it...

1. In Xcode, double-click on the `MyView.m` implementation file to open it.

2. In order for our view to receive keyboard events, it must be able to accept first responder status. Add the following method to the MyView class:

```
- (BOOL) acceptsFirstResponder {
  return YES;
}
```

3. We need to add the `keyDown:` method with the following code to implement the color changing logic to the MyView class:

```
- (void)keyDown:(NSEvent *)theEvent {
  NSString *letter = [theEvent characters];
  if ([letter isEqualToString:@"y"]) {
    fillColor = [NSColor yellowColor];
  } else if ([letter isEqualToString:@"r"]) {
    fillColor = [NSColor redColor];
  } else if ([letter isEqualToString:@"b"]) {
    fillColor = [NSColor blueColor];
  } else {
    fillColor = [NSColor whiteColor];
  }

  [self setNeedsDisplay:YES];
}
```

4. Choose **Build and Run** from the Xcode toolbar to run the application.

How it works...

In order for your custom view to receive keyboard events, it must be the first responder in the responder chain of the application. By implementing the `acceptsFirstResponder:` method and returning YES from this method, our view is ready to handle keyboard events in the `keyDown:` method. The `NSEvent` passed to the `keyDown:` method contains several properties that can be examined to determine information about the key down event. One of those properties, characters, will let you know which key was typed. You can also examine the `modifierFlags` property to determine if the *Shift, Command,* or *Control* key was also pressed when the event occurred.

There's more...

By implementing the `performKeyEquivalent:` method in your custom view, you can also override the default keyboard shortcuts. For example, *Command + T* will show the Font Chooser. We can implement `performKeyEquivalent:` and check that the event passed to us is for *Command + T* and provide some other functionality. For those keyboard shortcuts you do not handle, you must return the value by calling the super's `performKeyEquivalent:` method.

See also

The sample code and project for this recipe is located under the `KeyboardEvents` folder in the code bundled with this book.

Drawing strings with attributes

Attributed Strings allow you to draw text with formatting. You can provide attributes that describe such things as fonts, colors, shadows, and more. In this recipe we are going to use an `NSAttributedString` to draw a title for our custom view.

Getting ready

Let's build on the code from the previous recipe *Handling keyboard events In your view*. Using the Finder, duplicate the projects folder and name it `AttributedStrings`.

How to do it...

1. In Xcode, open the `MyView.m` file and add the following code at the end of the `drawRect:` method:

```
NSFont *font = [NSFont boldSystemFontOfSize:11.0];

NSArray *keys = [NSArray arrayWithObjects:NSFontAttributeName,
    NSForegroundColorAttributeName, nil];
NSArray *objects = [NSArray arrayWithObjects:font, [NSColor
    whiteColor], nil];
NSDictionary *attributes = s[NSDictionary
    dictionaryWithObjects:objects forKeys:keys];
NSAttributedString *attributedString = [[[NSAttributedString
alloc]
    initWithString:@"Packt Publishing" attributes:attributes]
    autorelease];
```

```
point = NSMakePoint((([self bounds].size.width / 2) -
    ([attributedString size].width / 2),
            ([self bounds].size.height - [middle size].height) +
                ([attributedString size].height / 2));
[attributedString drawAtPoint:point];
```

2. Choose **Build and Run** from Xcode's toolbar to run the application.

How it works...

In the title of our custom view, we are going to set the font and foreground color. We need to create two NSArrays, one to hold the keys and one to hold the values that make up the attributes for the attributed string. Next, we add the two arrays to an NSDictionary that we pass to the NSAttributedString initWithString: method. Finally, we draw the attributed string's title by subtracting the width of the title from the width of the title area.

There's more...

NSAttributedString supports twenty-three attributes you can set. Apple's reference document *NSAttributedString Application Kit Additions Reference* contains a description of each of these attribute constants. You can find this reference at the following location:
http://developer.apple.com/library/mac/#documentation/Cocoa/
Reference/ApplicationKit/Classes/NSAttributedString_AppKitAdditions/
Reference/Reference.html

See also

The sample code and project for this recipe is located under the AttributedStrings folder in the code bundled with this book.

3

Handling Events

In this chapter, we will cover:

- ▶ Interpreting the pinch gesture
- ▶ Interpreting the swipe gesture
- ▶ Interpreting the rotate gesture
- ▶ Handling special keys
- ▶ Working with NSResponder
- ▶ Application-wide notifications with NotificationCenter

Introduction

The trackpad is becoming more popular as an input device as all new Apple laptops now have a trackpad. Even desktop Macs have trackpad support with the addition of the Magic Trackpad. Adding gestures to your Cocoa application to support the trackpad is not difficult. The recipes in this chapter will show you how to add the three most popular gestures to your application.

We will also show you how to support function keys and other special keys on the users keyboard in your custom views. We will take a look at `NSResponder` and a few of the methods you should be familiar with to help you understand more about becoming a first responder. Our final recipe of this chapter will show you how to post and observe notifications within your application using the `NSNotificationCenter`.

 Some recipes in this chapter require Mac OS X Snow Leopard 10.6.

The Trackpad preferences allow you to easily adjust many gestures that will used in the following recipes.

 To make sure that your trackpad is recognizing gestures, make sure that you have set the correct preferences to enable gesture support under the Trackpad System Preference.

Interpreting the pinch gesture

The pinch gesture is a gesture normally used for the zooming of a view or for changing the font size of text. In this recipe, we will create a custom view that handles the pinch gesture to resize a custom view.

Getting ready

In Xcode, create a new Cocoa Application and name it `Pinch`.

How to do it...

1. In the Xcode project, right-click on the **Classes** folder and choose **Add...**, then choose **New File...** Under the **MacOS X** section, select **Cocoa Class**, then select **Objective-C** class. Finally, choose **NSView** in the **Subclass of** popup. Name the new file `MyView.m`

2. Double-click on the `MainMenu.xib` file in the Xcode project. From Interface Builders Library palette, drag a **Custom View** into the application window.

3. From Interface Builders Inspector's palette, select the **Identity** tab and set the **Class** popup to `MyView`.

4. Choose **Save** from the **File** menu to save the changes that you have made.

5. In Xcode, Add the following code in the `drawRect:` method of the `MyView` class implementation:

```
NSBezierPath *path = [NSBezierPath bezierPathWithRoundedRect:[self
    bounds] xRadius:8.0 yRadius:8.0];
[path setClip];

[[NSColor whiteColor] setFill];
[NSBezierPath fillRect:[self bounds]];

[path setLineWidth:3.0];

[[NSColor grayColor] setStroke];
[path stroke];
```

6. Next, we need to add the code to handle the pinch gesture. Add the following method to the `MyView` class implementation:

```
- (void)magnifyWithEvent:(NSEvent *)event {

    NSSize size = [self frame].size;
    size.height = size.height * ([event magnification] + 1.0);
    size.width = size.width * ([event magnification] + 1.0);

    [self setFrameSize:size];
}
```

7. Choose **Build and Run** from Xcode's toolbar to run the application.

How it works...

In our `drawRect:` method, we use Cocoa to draw a simple rounded rectangle with a three point wide gray stroke. Next, we implement the `magnifyWithEvent:` method. Because NSView inherits from NSResponder, we can override the `magnifyWithEvent:` method from the `NSResponder` class. When the user starts a pinch gesture, and the `magnifyWithEvent:` method is called, the `NSEvent` passed to us in the `magnifyWithEvent:` method which contains a magnification factor we can use to determine how much to scale our view. First, we get the current size of our view. We add one to the magnification factor and multiply by the frame's width and height to scale the view. Finally, we set the frame's new size.

There's more...

You will notice when running the sample code that our view resizes with the lower-left corner of our custom view remaining in a constant position. In order to make our view zoom in and out from the center, change the `magnifyWithEvent:` method's code to the following:

```
NSSize size = [self frame].size;
NSSize originalSize = size;
size.height = size.height * ([event magnification] + 1.0);
size.width = size.width * ([event magnification] + 1.0);

[self setFrameSize:size];

CGFloat deltaX = (originalSize.width - size.width) / 2;
CGFloat deltaY = (originalSize.height - size.height) / 2;

NSPoint origin = self.frame.origin;
origin.x = origin.x + deltaX;
origin.y = origin.y + deltaY;
[self setFrameOrigin:origin];
```

Basically, what we have done is moved our custom view's origin by the difference between the original size and the new size.

See also

The sample code and project for this recipe is located under the `Pinch` folder in the code bundled with this book.

Interpreting the swipe gesture

The swipe gesture is detected when three or more fingers move across the trackpad. This gesture is often used to page through a series of images. In this recipe, we will create a custom view that interprets the swipe gesture in four different directions and displays the direction of the swipe in our custom view:

Getting ready

In Xcode, create a new Cocoa Application and name it Swipe.

How to do it...

1. In the Xcode project, right-click on the **Classes** folder and choose **Add...**, then choose **New File...** Under the **MacOS X** section, select **Cocoa Class**, then select **Objective-C** class. Finally, choose **NSView** in the **Subclass of** popup. Name the new file MyView.m

2. Double-click on the MainMenu.xib file in the Xcode project. From Interface Builders Library palette, drag a **Custom View** into the application window.

3. From Interface Builders Inspector's palette, select the **Identity** tab and set the **Class** popup to MyView.

4. Choose **Save** from the **File** menu to save the changes that you have made.

5. In Xcode, open the MyView.h file and add the direction variable to the class interface:

   ```
   NSString *direction;
   ```

6. Open the MyView.m file and add the following code in the drawRect: method of the MyView class implementation:

   ```
   NSBezierPath *path = [NSBezierPath bezierPathWithRoundedRect:[self
      bounds] xRadius:8.0 yRadius:8.0];
   [path setClip];

   [[NSColor whiteColor] setFill];
   [NSBezierPath fillRect:[self bounds]];
   ```

```
[path setLineWidth:3.0];

[[NSColor grayColor] setStroke];
[path stroke];

if (direction == nil) {
  direction = @"";
}

NSAttributedString *string = [[[NSAttributedString alloc]
  initWithString:direction] autorelease];
NSPoint point = NSMakePoint(([self bounds].size.width / 2) -
  ([string size].width / 2), ([self bounds].size.height / 2) -
  ([string size].height / 2));
[string drawAtPoint:point];
```

7. Add the following code to handle the swipe gesture:

```
- (void)swipeWithEvent:(NSEvent *)event {
  if ([event deltaX] > 0) {
    direction = @"Left";
  } else if ([event deltaX] < 0) {
    direction = @"Right";
  } else if ([event deltaY] > 0) {
    direction = @"Up";
  } else if ([event deltaY] < 0){
    direction = @"Down";
  }

    [self setNeedsDisplay:YES];
}
```

8. In Xcode, choose **Build and Run** from the toolbar to run the application.

How it works...

As we did in the other recipes in this chapter, we draw a simple rounded rectangle in the drawRect: method of the view. However, we will also be drawing a string denoting the direction of the swipe in the middle of our view.

In order to handle the swipe gesture, we override the swipeWithEvent: method from the NSResponder class which NSView inherits. By inspecting the values of deltaX and deltaY of the NSEvent passed into the swipeWithEvent: method, we can determine the direction of the swipe. We set the direction string with the direction of the swipe so we can draw it in the drawRect: method. Finally, we call setNeedsDisplay:YES to force our view to redraw itself.

There's more...

You might have noticed that we do not need to override the `acceptsFirstResponder:` method in our view in order to handle the gesture events. When the mouse is located within our view, we automatically receive the gesture events. All we need to do is implement the methods for the gestures we are interested in.

See also

The sample code and project for this recipe is located under the `Swipe` folder in the code bundled with this book.

Interpreting the rotate gesture

The rotate gesture can be used in any number of ways in a custom view. From rotating the view itself or simulating a rotating dial in a custom control. This recipe will show you how to implement the rotate gesture to rotate a custom view. Using your thumb and index finger, you will be able to rotate the custom view around its center:

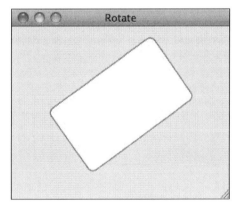

Getting ready

In Xcode, create a new Cocoa Application and name it `Rotate`.

How to do it...

1. In the Xcode project, right-click on the **Classes** folder and choose **Add...**, then choose **New File...** Under the **MacOS X** section, select **Cocoa Class**, then select **Objective-C** class. Finally, choose **NSView** in the **Subclass of** popup. Name the new file `MyView.m`.

2. Double-click on the `MainMenu.xib` file in the Xcode project. From Interface Builders Library palette, drag a **Custom View** into the application window.

3. From Interface Builders Inspector's palette, select the **Identity** tab and set the **Class** popup to `MyView`.

4. Choose **Save** from the **File** menu to save the changes that you have made.

5. In Xcode, Add the following code in the `drawRect:` method of the MyView class implementation:

```
NSBezierPath *path = [NSBezierPath bezierPathWithRoundedRect:[self
   bounds] xRadius:8.0 yRadius:8.0];
[path setClip];

[[NSColor whiteColor] setFill];
[NSBezierPath fillRect:[self bounds]];

[path setLineWidth:3.0];

[[NSColor grayColor] setStroke];
[path stroke];
```

6. Next we need to add the code to handle the rotate gesture. Add the following method to the MyView class implementation:

```
- (void)rotateWithEvent:(NSEvent *)event {
  CGFloat currentRotation = [self frameCenterRotation];
    [self setFrameCenterRotation:(currentRotation + [event
       rotation])];
}
```

7. Choose **Build and Run** from Xcode's toolbar to test the application.

How it works...

As we did in the previous recipe, we will create a simple rounded rectangle with a three-point stroke to represent our custom view.

Our custom view overrides the `rotateWithEvent:` method from `NSResponder` to handle the rotation gesture. The rotation property of the `NSEvent` passed to us in the `rotateWithEvent:` contains the change in rotation from the last time the `rotateWithEvent:` method was called. We simply add this value to our view's `frameCenterRotation` value to get the new rotation.

There's more...

The value returned from `NSEvent`'s rotation will be negative when the rotation is clockwise and positive when the rotation is counter-clockwise.

See also

The sample code and project for this recipe is located under the `Rotate` folder in the code bundled with this book.

Handling special keys

Depending on your application, you may need to handle keyboard shortcuts using the function keys or other special keys on the keyboard. In this recipe, we will show you how to handle these special keys in a custom view by overriding the `keyDown:` method.

Getting ready

In Xcode create a new Cocoa Application and name it `SpecialKeys`.

How to do it...

1. In the Xcode project, right-click on the **Classes** folder and choose **Add...**, then choose **New File...** Under the **MacOS X** section, select **Cocoa Class**, then select **Objective-C** class. Finally, choose **NSView** in the **Subclass of** popup. Name the new file `MyView.m`.

2. Click on the `MyView.h` file to open it and add the `message` variable to the MyView class interface:

   ```
   NSString *message;
   ```

3. Double-click on the `MainMenu.xib` file in the Xcode project. From Interface Builders Library palette, drag a **Custom View** into the application window.

4. From Interface Builders Inspector's palette, select the **Identity** tab and set the **Class** popup to `MyView`.

5. Choose **Save** from the **File** menu to save the changes that you have made.

6. In Xcode, click on `MyView.m` to open the MyView implementation.

7. Add the following `awakeFromNib:` method:

```
- (void) awakeFromNib {
  message = @"";
}
```

8. Next, add the code for the `drawRect:` method of the `MyView` class implementation:

```
NSBezierPath *path = [NSBezierPath bezierPathWithRect:[self
    bounds]];
[[NSColor whiteColor] set];
[path fill];

[[NSColor grayColor] set];
[path setLineWidth:3.0];
[path stroke];

NSAttributedString *attributedString = [[[NSAttributedString
    alloc] initWithString:message attributes:nil] autorelease];

NSPoint point = NSMakePoint(([self bounds].size.width / 2) -
    ([attributedString size].width / 2),
            ([self bounds].size.height / 2) - ([attributedString
    size].height / 2));
    [attributedString drawAtPoint:point];
```

9. Add the following `acceptsFirstResponder` method to `MyView.m`:

```
- (BOOL) acceptsFirstResponder {
  return YES;
}
```

10. Add the following `keyDown:` method to `MyView.m`:

```
- (void)keyDown:(NSEvent *)theEvent {

  if ([[theEvent characters] length] != 0) {
    NSString *characters = [theEvent characters];

    unichar key = [characters characterAtIndex:0];

    switch (key) {
      case NSF6FunctionKey:
        message = @"F6";
        break;
      case NSF7FunctionKey:
        message = @"F7";
```

```
    break;
case NSUpArrowFunctionKey:
  message = @"Up";
  break;
case NSDownArrowFunctionKey:
  message = @"Down";
  break;
case NSLeftArrowFunctionKey:
  message = @"Left";
  break;
case NSRightArrowFunctionKey:
  message = @"Right";
  break;
case NSDeleteFunctionKey: // Forward delete (fn + delete on
  laptop)
  message = @"Forward Delete";
  break;
case NSDeleteCharacter:
  message = @"Delete";
default:
  break;
    }
  }

  [self setNeedsDisplay:YES];
}
```

11. Choose **Build and Run** from Xcode's toolbar to run the application.

How it works...

First we will create a simple rectangle with a three-point stroke to represent our custom view.

Next, we override the `acceptsFirstResponder` method from `NSResponder` and return `YES`. This signals that we would like to be a first responder in the responder chain to handle keyboard events.

To handle the special keys on the keyboard, such as the function keys, we override the `keyDown:` method from the `NSResponder` class. In this method, we grab the first character from the passed `NSEvent`'s characters property. We then compare this `unichar` to Cocoa's predefined `NSFunctionKey`'s to handle the function key we are interested in. In our sample code, we display the special keys in our custom view, `MyView`, by using an `NSAttributedString`.

Lastly, we make a call to `setNeedsDisplay:YES` in order to redraw our view to show which special key was pressed.

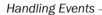

You can find a complete list of all the `NSFunctionKey`'s in Apple's documentation under the `NSEvent` Class Reference. Look under the heading "Function-Key Unicodes".

See also

The sample code and project for this recipe is located under the `SpecialKeys` folder in the code bundled with this book.

Working with NSResponder

Understanding how the responder chain works is important when building your own views with event handling. In this recipe, you will learn about `NSResponder`'s three most important methods and the sequence in which they are called.

Getting ready

In Xcode, create a new Cocoa Application and name it `NSResponder`.

How to do it...

1. In the Xcode project, right-click on the **Classes** folder and choose **Add...**, then choose **New File...** Under the **MacOS X** section, select **Cocoa Class**, then select **Objective-C** class. Finally, choose **NSView** in the **Subclass of** popup. Name the new file `MyView.m`.

2. In Xcode, Add the following code to the `drawRect:` method of the `MyView` class implementation:

```
NSBezierPath *path = [NSBezierPath bezierPathWithRoundedRect:[self
    bounds] xRadius:8.0 yRadius:8.0];
[path setClip];

[[NSColor whiteColor] setFill];
[NSBezierPath fillRect:[self bounds]];

[path setLineWidth:3.0];

[[NSColor grayColor] setStroke];
[path stroke];
```

3. Double-click on the `MainMenu.xib` file in the Xcode project. From the Interface Builders Library palette, drag a **TextField** into the application window.

4. In Interface Builder, drag a **Custom View** into the application window below the text field you just added.

5. Using the Inspector palette, select the **Identity** tab and select **MyView** from the **Class** popup.

6. Right-click on **Window (NSResponder)** and connect **initialFirstResponder** to the text field you dragged into the application window in step 3.

7. Next, right-click on the **TextField** and connect the **nextKeyView** to the **MyView Custom View**:

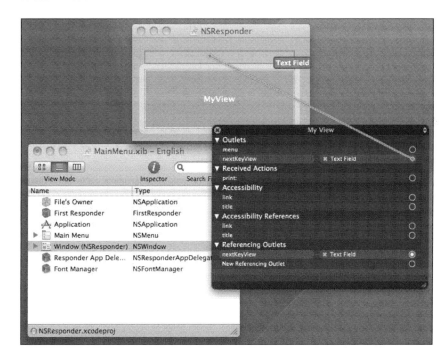

8. Right-click on the **MyView Custom View** and connect its **nextKeyView** to the **TextField**:

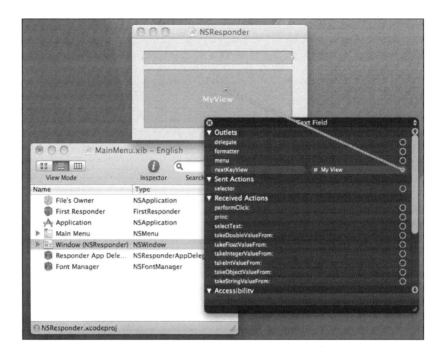

9. Choose **Save** from the **File** menu to save the changes that you have made:

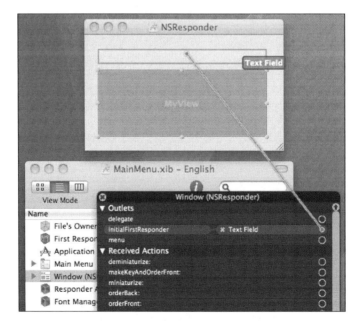

10. Back in Xcode, open the `MyView.m` file and add the following three methods to the `MyView` class implementation:

```
- (BOOL)acceptsFirstResponder {
  NSLog(@"acceptsFirstResponder");
   return YES;
}


- (BOOL)becomeFirstResponder {
  NSLog(@"becomeFirstResponder");
  return YES;
}


- (BOOL)resignFirstResponder {
  NSLog(@"resignFirstResponder");
  return YES;
}
```

11. Choose **Build and Run** from Xcode's toolbar to run the application.

How it works...

As we have done in the other recipes in this chapter, we start by creating a custom `NSView` called `MyView`. Our custom view overrides three methods from the `NSResponder` class to print the method names to the console when they are called.

When you run the code in this recipe, use the *Tab* key to move between the `NSTextField` and custom view. This will change the first responder and you will see the sequence of methods called the custom view becomes and resigns its first responder status.

There's more...

The three methods we have overridden from `NSResponder`, `acceptsFirstResponder`, `becomeFirstResponder`, and `resignFirstReponder` all return a `BOOL` value indicating whether or not our subclass has handled the first responder status. In this recipe, we have returned `YES` in all three methods. However, in some cases you may not want to resign the first responder status because the user has not completed entering some kind data. In this case, you would return NO until the user has entered the correct data.

Since this recipe's focus was `NSResponder`, you might like to know that `NSResponder` also defines the method `presentError:`, which when called with an `NSError` object will display an `NSAlert`. Calling this method will send the error up the responder chain. If no other responders handle the error, then `NSApp` will display the error message.

The sample code and project for this recipe is located under the NSResponder folder in the code bundled with this book.

Application-wide notifications with NotificationCenter

Using the NSNotificationCenter, you can send and receive notifications through your application using a simple publish and subscribe-like mechanism. Cocoa also makes use of notifications which you can observe to detect various changes. For example, when a user resizes a window, the NSWindowDidEndLiveResizeNotification notification will be posted to the notification center. Any of your classes can observe this notification and perform some action when the resizing of the window is complete.

In this recipe, we will send a notification when the application has finished launching. The notification will tell our custom view to change its color from white to red when it receives the notification.

Getting ready

In Xcode, create a new Cocoa Application and name it Notification.

How to do it...

1. In the XCode project, right-click on the **Classes** folder and choose **Add...**, then choose **New File...** Under the **MacOS X** section, select **Cocoa Class**, then select **Objective-C** class. Finally, choose **NSView** in the **Subclass of** popup. Name the new file MyView.m.

2. In Xcode, click on the NotificationAppDelegate.m file and add the following code in the applicationDidFinishLaunching method:

    ```
    NSDictionary *dictionary = [NSDictionary
      dictionaryWithObject:[NSColor redColor] forKey:@"fillColor"];

    NSNotificationCenter *notificationCenter = [NSNotificationCenter
      defaultCenter];
    [notificationCenter postNotificationName:@"ColorChange"
      object:self userInfo:dictionary];
    ```

3. Click on MyView.h to open it and add the color variable to the class interface:

    ```
    NSColor *color;
    ```

4. Click on `MyView.m` to open it and change the `initWithFrame:` method so that it looks like this:

```
- (id)initWithFrame:(NSRect)frame {
  self = [super initWithFrame:frame];
  if (self) {
    color = [NSColor whiteColor];

    NSNotificationCenter *notificationCenter = [NSNotificationCenter
      defaultCenter];
    [notificationCenter addObserver:self
      selector:@selector(handleColorChange:) name:@"ColorChange"
      object:nil];
    }
  return self;
}
```

5. Add the following code in the `drawRect:` method of the `MyView` class implementation:

```
NSBezierPath *path = [NSBezierPath bezierPathWithRect:[self
  bounds]];
[color set];
[path fill];

[[NSColor grayColor] set];
[path setLineWidth:3.0];
[path stroke];
```

6. Add the following method to the `MyView` class implementation:

```
- (void) handleColorChange:(NSNotification *)notification {
  NSLog(@"Received notification");

  NSDictionary *dictionary = [notification userInfo];
  color = [dictionary objectForKey:@"fillColor"];

  [self setNeedsDisplay:YES];
}
```

7. Add the following `dealloc` method to the `MyView` class:

```
- (void)dealloc {
  [[NSNotificationCenter defaultCenter] removeObserver:self];

  [super dealloc];
}
```

8. Double-click on `MainMenu.xib` to open the file in Interface Builder.

9. Drag a **Custom View** from Interface Builder's Library palette into the application window.

10. Using the Inspector palette, select the **Identity** tab and select **MyView** from the **Class** popup.

11. Choose **Save** from the **File** menu to save the changes that you have made.

12. Click on **Build and Run** on Xcode's toolbar to run the application.

How it works...

When the application has finished launching, it will send a `ColorChange` notification through the default notification center with the color red.

In our custom view, which is just a white filled rectangle with a gray border, we add ourselves as an observer in the default notification center observing the `ColorChange` notification. We also specify that the `setColor:` method should be called when we receive the notification.

In the `setColor:` method of our view, we pull the color out of the notification and set the color property of our view. We then call the `setNeedsDisplay:YES` method to force our view to redraw with the new color.

Finally, we remove our view from the notification center when our view is deallocated.

There's more...

Cocoa also provides an `NSDistributedNotificationCenter` class to pass notifications between applications. For more information see Apple's companion guide *Notification Programming Topics*.

See also

The sample code and project for this recipe is located under the `Notification` folder in the code bundled with this book.

4
Using Animation

In this chapter, we will cover:

- ▶ Understanding the CALayer class
- ▶ Animation by changing properties
- ▶ Using animation to swap views
- ▶ Using the flip animation
- ▶ Using a CAAnimationGroup
- ▶ Using Keyframe animations
- ▶ Using CAMediaTiming in animations

Introduction

Layers are a very powerful way to draw or animate your views. Using layer-backed views is similar to using layers in a graphics application like Adobe's Photoshop. Layers can be stacked and animated to create powerful effects.

 Some recipes in this chapter require Mac OS X Snow Leopard 10.6.

Understanding the CALayer class

In this recipe, we will use multiple layers to draw our custom view. Using a delegate method, we will draw the background of our view. A second layer will be used to include an image centered in the view. When complete, the sample application will resemble the following screenshot:

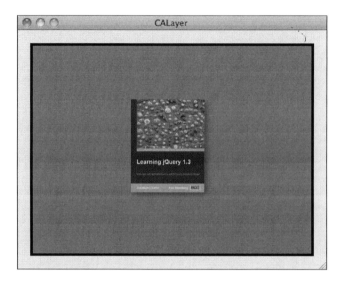

Getting ready

In Xcode, create a new Cocoa Application and name it CALayer.

How to do it...

1. In the Xcode project, right-click on the **Classes** folder and choose **Add...**, then choose **New File...** Under the **MacOS X** section, select **Cocoa Class**, then select **Objective-C** class. Finally, choose **NSView** in the **Subclass of** popup. Name the new file MyView.m.

2. In the Xcode project, expand the **Frameworks** group and then expand **Other Frameworks**. Right-click on **Other Frameworks** and choose **Add...**, then choose **Existing Frameworks...** Find **QuartzCore.framework** in the list of frameworks and choose **Add**.

3. Click on MyView.m to open it and add the following import:

    ```
    #import <QuartzCore/QuartzCore.h>
    ```

4. Remove the `initWithFrame:` and `drawRect:` methods.

5. Add the following `awakeFromNib` method:

```
- (void) awakeFromNib {
  CALayer *largeLayer = [CALayer layer];
  [largeLayer setName:@"large"];
  [largeLayer setDelegate:self];
  [largeLayer setBounds:[self bounds]];
  [largeLayer setBorderWidth:4.0];
  [largeLayer setLayoutManager:[CAConstraintLayoutManager
    layoutManager]];


  CALayer *smallLayer = [CALayer layer];
  [smallLayer setName:@"small"];
  CGImageRef image = [self convertImage:[NSImage
    imageNamed:@"LearningJQuery"]];
  [smallLayer setBounds:CGRectMake(0, 0, CGImageGetWidth(image),
    CGImageGetHeight(image))];
  [smallLayer setContents:(id)image];
  [smallLayer addConstraint:[CAConstraint
    constraintWithAttribute:kCAConstraintMidY
                            relativeTo:@"superlayer"
                             attribute:kCAConstraintMidY]];

  [smallLayer addConstraint:[CAConstraint
    constraintWithAttribute:kCAConstraintMidX
                            relativeTo:@"superlayer"
                             attribute:kCAConstraintMidX]];

  CFRelease(image);

  [largeLayer addSublayer:smallLayer];
  [largeLayer setNeedsDisplay];

  [self setLayer:largeLayer];
  [self setWantsLayer:YES];
}
```

6. Add the following two methods to the `MyView` class as well:

```
- (void)drawLayer:(CALayer *)layer inContext:(CGContextRef)context
{

    CGContextSetRGBFillColor(context, .5, .5, .5, 1);
    CGContextFillRect(context, [layer bounds]);
}


- (CGImageRef) convertImage:(NSImage *)image {
    CGImageSourceRef source = CGImageSourceCreateWithData((CFDataRef
) [image TIFFRepresentation],
        NULL);
    CGImageRef imageRef = CGImageSourceCreateImageAtIndex(source, 0,
        NULL);
    CFRelease(source);

    return imageRef;
}
```

7. Open the `MyView.h` file and add the following method declaration:

```
- (CGImageRef) convertImage:(NSImage *)image;
```

8. Right-click on the `CALayer` project in Xcode's project view and choose **Add...**, then choose **Existing Files....** Choose the `LearningJQuery.jpg` image and click **Add**.

9. Double-click on the `MainMenu.xib` file in the Xcode project. From Interface Builder's Library palette, drag a **Custom View** into the application window.

10. From Interface Builder's Inspectors palette, select the **Identity** tab and set the **Class** popup to `MyView`.

11. Back in Xcode, choose **Build and Run** from the toolbar to run the application.

How it works...

We are creating two layers for our view. The first layer is a large layer, which will be the same size as our `MyView` view. We set the large layers delegate to `self` so that we can draw the layer in the `drawLayer:` delegate method. The `drawLayer:` delegate method simply fills the layer with a mid-gray color. Next, we set the bounds property and a border width property on the larger layer.

Next, we create a smaller layer whose contents will be the image that we included in the project. We also add a layout manager to this layer and configure the constraints of the layout manager to keep the smaller layer centered both horizontally and vertically relative to the larger view using the `superlayer` keyword.

Lastly, we set the small layer as a sub-layer of the large layer and force a redraw of the large layer by calling `setNeedsDisplay`. Next, we set the large layer as the `MyView`'s layer. We also need to call the `setWantsLayer:YES` on the `MyView` to enable the use of layers in our view.

There's more...

Since we used a layout manager to center the image in the view, the layout manager will also handle the centering of the image when the user resizes the view or window. To see this in action, modify the Size properties in Interface Builder for the custom view as shown in the screenshot below:

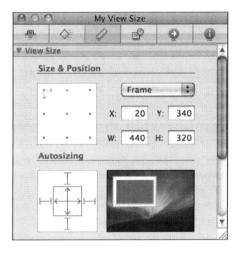

See also

The sample code and project for this recipe is located under the `CALayer` folder in the code bundled with this book.

Animation by changing properties

Cocoa provides a way to animate views by changing properties using implied animations. In this recipe, we will resize our custom view when the resize button is clicked, by changing the views frame size.

Getting ready

In Xcode, create a new Cocoa Application and name it `ChangingProperties`.

How to do it...

1. In the Xcode project, right-click on the **Classes** folder and choose **Add...**, then choose **New File...** Under the **MacOS X** section, select **Cocoa Class**, then select **Objective-C** class. Finally, choose **NSView** from the **Subclass of** popup. Name the new file `MyView.m`.

2. Click on the `MyView.m` file to open it and add the following in the `drawRect:` method:

```
NSBezierPath *path = [NSBezierPath bezierPathWithRoundedRect:[self
    bounds] xRadius:8.0 yRadius:8.0];
[path setClip];

[[NSColor whiteColor] setFill];
[NSBezierPath fillRect:[self bounds]];

[path setLineWidth:3.0];

[[NSColor grayColor] setStroke];
[path stroke];
```

3. Click on the `ChangingPropertiesAppDelegate.h` to open it.

4. Next, insert an import for the `MyView.h` header file:

```
#import "MyView.h"
```

5. Add the following variables to the class interface:

```
NSButton *button;
MyView *myView;
```

6. Add the following properties to the class interface:

```
@property (assign) IBOutlet NSButton *button;
@property (assign) IBOutlet MyView *myView;
```

7. Add the method declaration for when the Resize button is clicked:

```
- (IBAction) resizeButtonHit:(id)sender;
```

8. Click on the `ChangingPropertiesAppDelegate.m` file to open it.

9. Add our synthesized variables below the synthesized window variable:

```
@synthesize button;
@synthesize myView;
```

10. Create a global static boolean for tracking the size of the view:

```
static BOOL isSmall = YES;
```

11. Add the `resizeButtonHit:` method to the class implementation:

```
- (IBAction) resizeButtonHit:(id)sender {
  NSRect small = NSMakeRect(20, 250, 150, 90);
  NSRect large = NSMakeRect(20, 100, 440, 240);

  if (isSmall == YES) {
    [[myView animator] setFrame:large];
    isSmall = NO;
  } else {
    [[myView animator] setFrame:small];
    isSmall = YES;
  }
}
```

12. Double-click on the `MainMenu.xib` file in the Xcode project. From Interface Builders Library palette, drag a **Custom View** into the application window.

13. From Interface Builder's Inspector's palette, select the **Identity** tab and set the **Class** popup to `MyView`.

14. From the Library palette, drag a **Push Button** into the application window.

15. Adjust the layout of the Custom View and button so that it resembles the screenshot below:

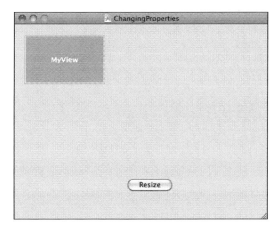

16. From Interface Builder's Inspector's palette, select the **Identity** tab and set the **Class** popup to **MyView**.

17. Right-click on the **Changing Properties App Delegate** so that you can connect the outlets to the **MyView** Custom View, the **Resize** Push Button, and the **resizeButtonHit** action:

18. Back in Xcode, choose **Build and Run** from the toolbar to run the application.

How it works...

We define two sizes for our view, one small size that is the same as the initial size of the view, and one large size. Depending on the state of the isSmall global variable, we set the view's frame size to one of our predefined sizes. Note that we set the view's frame via the views animator property. By using this property, we make use of the implicit animations available in the view.

There's more...

Using the same technique, we can animate several other properties of the view such as its position or opacity. For more information on which properties can be implicitly animated, see Apple's *Core Animation Programming Guide*.

See also

The sample code and project for this recipe is located under the ChangingProperties folder in the code bundled with this book.

Using animation to swap views

One use of animation in Cocoa applications is to change views. In this recipe, we will create two views and swap them using a transition to slide the new view in from the left, replacing the existing view.

Getting ready

In Xcode, create a new Cocoa Application and name it `Swap`.

How to do it...

1. In the Xcode project, right-click on the **Classes** folder and choose **Add...**, then choose **New File...** Under the **MacOS X** section, select **Cocoa Class**, then select **Objective-C** class. Finally, choose **NSView** in the **Subclass of** popup. Name the new file `MyView.m`.

2. In the project view, expand the **Frameworks** group and then expand **Other Frameworks**. Right-click on **Other Frameworks** and choose **Add...**, then choose **Existing Frameworks...** Find **QuartzCore.framework** in the list of frameworks and choose **Add**.

3. Click on the `SwapAppDelegate.h` file to open it and add the following import:

    ```
    #import "MyView.h"
    ```

4. Add the following variables to the `SwapAppDelegate` class interface after the window variable:

    ```
    NSButton *button;
    MyView *myView;
    NSView *nameView;
    NSView *emailView;
    NSString *currentView;
    ```

5. Add the following properties below the property for the window variable:

    ```
    @property (retain, nonatomic) IBOutlet NSButton *button;
    @property (retain, nonatomic) IBOutlet MyView *myView;
    @property (retain, nonatomic) IBOutlet NSView *nameView;
    @property (retain, nonatomic) IBOutlet NSView *emailView;
    ```

6. We need to add the following method declaration to the class interface

    ```
    - (IBAction) swapButtonHit:(id)sender;
    ```

7. Open the `SwapAppDelegate.m` file and add an import for QuartzCore:

    ```
    #import <QuartzCore/QuartzCore.h>
    ```

8. We need to synthesize the variables that we added to the class interface. Below the window variable's synthesize statement, add the following:

    ```
    @synthesize button;
    @synthesize myView;
    @synthesize nameView;
    @synthesize emailView;
    ```

9. In the `applicationDidFinishLaunching` method add the following code:

    ```
    currentView = @"nameView";
    [myView addSubview:nameView];
    ```

10. Next, add the `swapButtonHit:` method:

    ```
    - (IBAction) swapButtonHit:(id)sender {
      if ([currentView isEqualToString:@"nameView"] == YES) {
        [[myView animator] replaceSubview:nameView with:emailView];
        currentView = @"emailView";
      } else {
        [[myView animator] replaceSubview:emailView with:nameView];
        currentView = @"nameView";
      }
    }
    ```

11. Click on the `MyView.m` file to open it and add the following imports:

    ```
    #import "MyView.h"
    #import <QuartzCore/QuartzCore.h>
    ```

12. Add the following `awakeFromNib` method:

    ```
    - (void) awakeFromNib {
      [self setWantsLayer:YES];

      CATransition *transition = [CATransition animation];
      [transition setDuration:1.0];
      [transition setType:kCATransitionPush];
      [transition setSubtype:kCATransitionFromLeft];

      NSDictionary *dictionary = [NSDictionary
        dictionaryWithObject:transition forKey:@"subviews"];
        [self setAnimations:dictionary];
    }
    ```

13. Double-click on the `MainMenu.xib` file to open it in Interface Builder.

14. From Interface Builders library palette, drag a **Custom View** into the application window.

15. Using the Inspectors palette, choose the **Identity** tab and set the **Class** to `MyView`.

16. From the Inspectors palette, choose the **Size** tab to resize the view. Make the view 480 pixels in width and 360 pixels in height.

17. You will also need to drag a **Push Button** into the window.

18. Your layout should resemble the following screenshot:

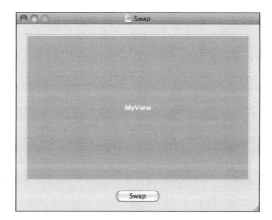

19. Next, we need to add two **Custom Views** from the Library palette to the `MainMenu.xib` project window.

20. Rename the first view from **Custom View** to **Name**.

21. Change the second view's name to **Email**.

22. Your `MainMenu.xib` project window should resemble the following:

23. Double-click on the Name view that you just added to open it.

24. Using the **Size** tab on the Inspector palette, set the view's size to 480 pixels in width and 280 pixels in height.

25. From the Library palette, drag some labels and text fields into the view so that it resembles the following screenshot:

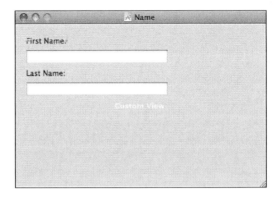

26. Double-click on the Email view that you just added to open it.

27. Using the **Size** tab on the Inspector palette, set the views size to 480 pixels in width and 280 pixels in height.

28. From the Library palette, drag some labels and text fields into the view so that it resembles the following screenshot:

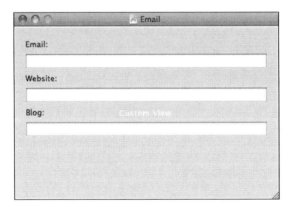

29. From the MainMenu.xib project window, double-click on the **Window (Swap)** item to open it.

30. Right-click on the Swap App Delegate to show the outlet connections window:

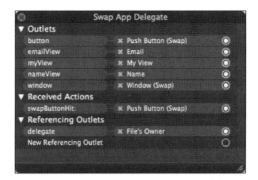

31. Drag a connection from the **button** outlet to the **Push Button** in the application window.

32. Drag a connection from the **emailView** outlet to the **Email** `NSView` in the `MainMenu.xib` project window.

33. Drag a connection from the **myView** outlet to the **MyView** view in the application window.

34. Drag a connection from the **nameView** outlet to the **Name** `NSView` in the `MainMenu.xib` project window.

35. Back in Xcode, choose **Build and Run** from the toolbar to run the application.

How it works...

First, we set up our `MyView` as a placeholder for where the views will be swapped. The `MyView` class sets up a `CATransition` in its `awakeFromNib` method using a `kCATransitionPush` type and a `kCATransitionFromLeft` subtype. Also note that we call `setWantsLayer:YES` to enable layers in the `MyView` class.

Next, we create a dictionary of animations containing our transition animation. We then set the dictionary as the view's animations.

Finally, in the `SwapAppDelegate` class's `swapButtonHit:` method, we use the `currentView` variable to determine which view is currently displaying. We then call `myView`'s `replaceSubview` method using the animator property, which sets our animation in action.

There's more...

The CATransition animation supports four types and subtypes that can be used to alter the transition effect. The four supported types are kCATransitionFade, kCATransitionMoveIn, kCATransitionPush, and kCATransitionReveal. The following subtypes are supported: kCATransitionFromRight, kCATransitionFromLeft, kCATransitionFromTop, and kCATransitionFromBottom.

See also

The sample code and project for this recipe is located under the Swap folder in the code bundled with this book.

Using the flip animation

In this recipe, we will use the transform property to animate the flipping of a views layer.

Getting ready

In Xcode, create a new Cocoa Application and name it Flip.

How to do it...

1. In the Xcode project, right-click on the **Classes** folder and choose **Add...**, then choose **New File...** Under the **MacOS X** section, select **Cocoa Class**, then select **Objective-C** class. Finally, choose **NSView** in the **Subclass of** popup. Name the new file MyView.m.

2. Right-click on the Flip project icon in Xcode's project view. Choose **Add...**, then choose **Existing Files...**. Navigate to /Library/Desktop Pictures/Aqua Graphite. jpg and choose **Add**.

3. Click on MyView.m to open the MyView implementation.

4. You can safely remove the initWithFrame: and drawRect: methods.

5. Add the following awakeFromNib method:

```
- (void) awakeFromNib {
  CALayer *layer = [CALayer layer];

  CGImageRef image = [self convertImage:[NSImage imageNamed:@"Aqua
    Graphite"]];

  layer.anchorPoint = CGPointMake(0.5, 0.5);
  layer.contents = (id)image;
```

```
    layer.borderWidth = 1.0;

    CFRelease(image);

    [self setLayer:layer];
    [self setWantsLayer:YES];
}
```

6. We need to add the following method to convert our NSImage to a CGImageRef:

```
- (CGImageRef) convertImage:(NSImage *)image {
    CGImageSourceRef source = CGImageSourceCreateWithData((CFDataRef
) [image TIFFRepresentation],
    NULL);
    CGImageRef imageRef = CGImageSourceCreateImageAtIndex(source, 0,
      NULL);
    CFRelease(source);

    return imageRef;
}
```

7. Click on MyView.h to open the MyView class interface.

8. Add the following method declaration for our convertImage method:

```
- (CGImageRef) convertImage:(NSImage *)image;
```

9. In the project view, expand the **Frameworks** group and then expand **Other Frameworks**. Right-click on **Other Frameworks** and choose **Add...**, then choose **Existing Frameworks...** Find **QuartzCore.framework** in the list of frameworks and choose **Add**.

10. Click on the FlipAppDelegate.h file to open the file.

11. Add an import for the MyView class:

```
#import "MyView.h"
```

12. Next, we need to add a few variables to the MyView class. Add the following variables below the window variable:

```
MyView *myView;
NSButton *button;
BOOL forward;
```

13. Add the following properties for the myView and button variables:

```
@property (assign) IBOutlet MyView *myView;
@property (assign) IBOutlet NSButton *button;
```

14. We need to add two method declarations for the methods in the `MyView` class implementation:

```
- (IBAction) performFlip:(id)sender;
CGFloat DegreesToRadians(CGFloat degrees);
```

15. Click on `FlipAppDelegate.m` to open the file.

16. Add an import for QuartzCore:

```
#import <QuartzCore/QuartzCore.h>
```

17. Add a synthesize statement for the `myView` and `button` variables:

```
@synthesize myView;
@synthesize button;
```

18. Next, we need to add the `performFlip:` method:

```
- (IBAction) performFlip:(id)sender {
  CALayer *layer = [myView layer];

  [CATransaction setValue:[NSNumber numberWithFloat:2.0f]
          forKey:kCATransactionAnimationDuration];

  if (forward == NO) {
    layer.transform =
      CATransform3DMakeRotation(DegreesToRadians(180), 0.0f, 1.0f,
      0.0f);
  } else {
    layer.transform =
      CATransform3DMakeRotation(DegreesToRadians(0), 0.0f, 1.0f,
      0.0f);
  }

  forward = forward == NO ? YES : NO;
}
```

19. Add our utility method to convert degrees to radians:

```
CGFloat DegreesToRadians(CGFloat degrees)
{
  return degrees * M_PI / 180;
}
```

20. Double-click on `MainMenu.xib` to open the file in Interface Builder.

21. From the Library palette in Interface Builder, drag a **Custom View** to the application window.

22. Using the **Size** tab in the Inspector palette set the size of the custom view to 440 pixels in width and 192 pixels in height.

23. Select the Identity tab in the Inspector palette and set the **Class** to MyView

24. Drag a **Push Button** from the Library palette to the application window. Change its title to **Flip**.

25. Your layout should resemble the screenshot below:

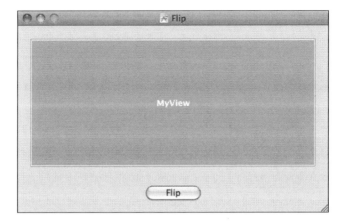

26. From the `MainMenu.xib` project window, right-click on the **Flip App Delegate** to connect the outlets and actions.

27. Drag a connection from the **button** outlet to the **Push Button**.

28. Drag a connection from the **myView** outlet to the **MyView Custom View**.

29. Finally, drag a connection from the **performFlip:** action to the **Push Button**.

30. When finished, your connections should look similar to those shown below:

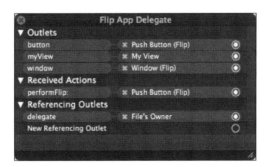

31. Back in Xcode, choose **Build and Run** to run the application.

How it works...

In the `awakeFromNib` method of the `MyView` class, we create a layer whose contents will contain the image that we added to the project from the `Desktop Pictures` folder. Note that we need to convert the `NSImage` to a `CGImageRef`, which the contents property of the layer will be expecting. We also set the layers anchor point to the center of the layer and add a one point black border around the layer. Next, we set the layer as the `MyView`'s layer and we call `setWantsLayer:YES` on the view.

When the Flip button is clicked, it invokes our `performFlip:` method in the `FlipAppDelegate`. Here we get the view's layer and set the transform property to a `CATransform3DMakeRotation` transform. Because the transform expects radians, we use our utility method to convert degrees to radians. Since we are rotating the y axis, we set the x and z axis to 0.0 and the y axis to 1.0.

There's more...

The default duration for animations is one second. This seems to be a little fast for the flip animation. In the `performFlip:` method, we adjust the duration to two seconds using the `kCATransactionAnimationDuration` property.

See also

The sample code and project for this recipe is located under the `Flip` folder in the code bundled with this book.

Using a CAAnimationGroup

In this recipe, we will group multiple animations together and run them on our view's layer.

Getting ready

In Xcode, create a new Cocoa Application and name it `AnimationGroup`.

How to do it...

1. In the Xcode project, right-click on the **Classes** folder and choose **Add...**, then choose **New File...** Under the **MacOS X** section select **Cocoa Class**, then select **Objective-C** class. Finally, choose **NSView** in the **Subclass of** popup. Name the new file `MyView.m`.

2. Click on `MyView.m` to open the file.

3. Add the following `awakeFromNib` method:

```
- (void) awakeFromNib {
    [self setWantsLayer:YES];
}
```

4. In the `drawRect:` method, add the following code:

```
NSBezierPath *path = [NSBezierPath bezierPathWithRoundedRect:[self
    bounds] xRadius:8.0 yRadius:8.0];
[path setClip];

[[NSColor whiteColor] setFill];
[NSBezierPath fillRect:[self bounds]];

[path setLineWidth:3.0];

[[NSColor grayColor] setStroke];
[path stroke];
```

5. Click on the `AnimationGroupAppDelegate.h` to open it and add an import for the `MyView` class header file:

```
#import "MyView.h"
```

6. Add the following variables to the delegate's class interface:

```
NSButton *button;
MyView *myView;
```

7. We need to add some properties for the new variables. Add these properties below the `NSWindow` property:

```
@property (assign) IBOutlet NSButton *button;
@property (assign) IBOutlet MyView *myView;
```

8. Finally, add the method declaration for the `buttonHit:` method:

```
- (IBAction) buttonHit:(id)sender;
```

9. Click on the `AnimationGroupAppDelegate.m` to open it.

10. Add an import for QuartzCore:

```
#import <QuartzCore/QuartzCore.h>
```

11. In the project view, expand the **Frameworks** group and then expand **Other Frameworks**. Right-click on **Other Frameworks** and choose **Add...**, then choose **Existing Frameworks...** Find **QuartzCore.framework** in the list of frameworks and choose **Add**.

12. Synthesize the `button` and `myView` variables:

```
@synthesize button;
@synthesize myView;
```

13. Finally, add the following `buttonHit:` method:

```
- (IBAction) buttonHit:(id)sender {
  CABasicAnimation *fadeAnimation = [CABasicAnimation
    animationWithKeyPath:@"opacity"];
  [fadeAnimation setAutoreverses:YES];
  [fadeAnimation setToValue:[NSNumber numberWithFloat:0.0]];

  CABasicAnimation *scaleAnimation = [CABasicAnimation
    animationWithKeyPath:@"transform.scale"];
  [scaleAnimation setAutoreverses:YES];
  [scaleAnimation setToValue:[NSNumber numberWithFloat:0.0]];

  CATransform3D transform = CATransform3DMakeRotation(M_PI, 0.0f,
    1.0f, 0.0f);
  CABasicAnimation *rotateAnimation = [CABasicAnimation
    animationWithKeyPath:@"transform.rotation"];
  [rotateAnimation setToValue:[NSValue
    valueWithCATransform3D:transform]];

  NSArray *animations = [NSArray arrayWithObjects:fadeAnimation,
    scaleAnimation, rotateAnimation, nil];

  CAAnimationGroup *animationGroup = [CAAnimationGroup animation];
  [animationGroup setDuration:5.0];
  [animationGroup setRepeatCount: 1e100f];
  [animationGroup setAnimations:animations];

  [[myView layer] addAnimation:animationGroup forKey:@"fadeAndRota
te"];
}
```

14. Double-click on the `MainMenu.xib` file to open it in Interface Builder.

15. From the Library palette, drag a **Custom View** into the application window.

16. Using the Identity tab on the Inspector palette, set the Custom View's **Class** to **MyView**.

17. We will need a button to start the animation, so drag a **Push Button** into the application window. Set the buttons title to **Animate**.

18. The final application window layout should look similar to the following screenshot:

19. Next, we need to connect our outlets and actions. Right-click on the **Animation Group App Delegate** from the `MainMenu.xib` project window to display the outlets window:

20. Drag a connection from the **button** outlet to the "**Animate**" **Push Button** in the application window.

21. Drag a connection from the **myView** outlet to the **MyView** Custom View.

22. Finally, drag a connection from the `buttonHit:` action to the "**Animate**" **Push Button** in the application window.

23. Back in Xcode, choose **Build and Run** to run the application.

How it works...

As we have done in other recipes, we create a simple custom view, which we will animate. When the `buttonHit:` method is called, we create two basic animations. In the first animation, we adjust the opacity of the view's layer from its current value to 0.0. The second animation will modify the view layer's scale to a value of 0.0. Finally, our last animation will rotate the view layer.

In order to group the animations, we add them to an `NSArray` so we can later add them to the `CAAnimationGroup`. Next, we create the `CAAnimationGroup`, set its duration to five seconds, and set it to repeat forever. Finally, we set our array of animations and add our animation group to the view's layer, which starts the animation.

There's more...

When animations are added to an animation group, the individual animation's delegates, if set, will not be called. Also note, the `removedOnCompletion` property of the individual animations will be ignored when used in an animation group.

See also

The sample code and project for this recipe is located under the `AnimationGroup` folder in the code bundled with this book.

Using Keyframe animations

In this recipe, we will create a Keyframe animation to animate the position of a button over a path.

Getting ready

In Xcode, create a new Cocoa Application and name it `Keyframe`.

How to do it...

1. In the project view, expand the **Frameworks** group and then expand **Other Frameworks**. Right-click on **Other Frameworks** and choose **Add...**, then choose **Existing Frameworks...** Find **QuartzCore.framework** in the list of frameworks and choose **Add**.

2. Click on `KeyFrameAppDelegate.h` to open it.

3. Add a variable for the `NSButton` in the class interface:

   ```
   NSButton *button;
   ```

4. Next, add a property for the `button` variable we just added:

   ```
   @property (assign) IBOutlet NSButton *button;
   ```

5. Finally, add the following to method declarations:

   ```
   - (void) animationButtonHit:(id)sender;
   - (CGPathRef) createPath;
   ```

6. Click on the `KeyFrameAppDelegate.m` file to open it.

7. First, we need to add an import for QuartzCore:

   ```
   #import <QuartzCore/QuartzCore.h>
   ```

8. Add the synthesize statement for the `button` variable:

   ```
   @synthesize button;
   ```

9. Add the following code to the `applicationDidFinishLaunching:` method:

   ```
   [[button superview] setWantsLayer:YES];
   ```

10. Next, add the following code, which defines the `animationButtonHit:` method:

    ```
    - (void) animationButtonHit:(id)sender {
      CGPathRef path = [self createPath];

      CAKeyframeAnimation *animation = [CAKeyframeAnimation
        animation];
      [animation setPath:path];
      [animation setDuration:4];
      [animation setRepeatCount:1];
      [animation setRemovedOnCompletion:YES];
      [[button layer] addAnimation:animation forKey:@"position"];

      CGPathRelease(path);
    }
    ```

11. Finally, add the following method to define the path of the animation:

    ```
    - (CGPathRef) createPath
    {
      CGFloat kMargin = 14.0;

      NSSize size = [button bounds].size;
      NSPoint position = [button frame].origin;
      NSRect frame = [[button window] frame];

        CGMutablePathRef path = CGPathCreateMutable();

      CGPathMoveToPoint(path, NULL, position.x, position.y);
      CGPathAddLineToPoint(path, NULL, kMargin, kMargin);
      CGPathAddLineToPoint(path, NULL, (frame.size.width - kMargin) -
        size.width , kMargin);
      CGPathAddLineToPoint(path, NULL, (frame.size.width - kMargin) -
        size.width, position.y);
      CGPathAddLineToPoint(path, NULL, position.x, position.y);

      return path;
    }
    ```

12. Double-click on the `MainMenu.xib` file to open it in Interface Builder.

13. Using the **Size** tab on the Inspector's palette, set the size of the application window to a width of 400 pixels and a height of 300 pixels.

14. From the Library palette, drag a **Push Button** to the application window. Using the **Size** tab on the Inspector's palette, set the button's X position to 14 and its Y position to 284.

15. Right-click on the `Keyframe App Delegate` in the `MainWindow.xib` project window to display the outlet connection window:

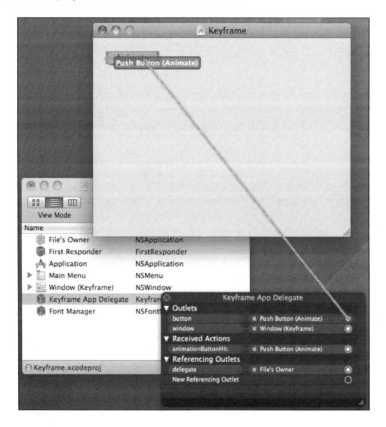

16. Drag a connection from the **button** outlet to the **Push Button** in the application window.

17. Drag a connection from the **animationButtonHit:** action to the **Push Button** in the application window.

18. Back in Xcode, choose **Build and Run** from the toolbar to run the application.

How it works...

When the application finishes launching, we call `setWantsLayer:YES` on the button's superview in order to enable layers on the button view.

Before we create the key frame animation, we build a `CGPathRef`. Our path will be built using the windows frame with an inset of fourteen pixels. The path is made up of four segments, which will represent our frames in the key frame animation.

Next, we create a key frame animation setting the path, and a duration of four seconds. We set the animation to repeat once. We also set the `removedOnCompletion` property to `YES` in order to remove the animation from the layer when it completes.

Finally, we add our animation to the buttons layer to start the animation.

There's more...

When using a path in a key frame animation, you can also set a rotation mode to specify how an object rotates as it moves over the path. Currently, there are two values that can be set for the rotation mode. The first, `kCAAnimationRotateAuto`, specifies that the animated object move along a tangent or just touching the path. The second value, `kCAAnimationRotateAutoReverse` directs the object to rotate at a 180 degree tangent to the path.

See also

The sample code and project for this recipe is located under the `Keyframe` folder in the code bundled with this book.

Using CAMediaTiming in animations

In this recipe, we use a timing function from the `CAMediaTiming` class to set the pace of an animation.

Getting ready

In Xcode, create a new Cocoa Application and name it `MediaTiming`.

How to do it...

1. In the Xcode project, right-click on the **Classes** folder and choose **Add...**, then choose **New File...** Under the **MacOS X** section, select **Cocoa Class**, then select **Objective-C** class. Finally, choose **NSView** in the **Subclass of** popup. Name the new file `MyView.m`.

2. Click on `MyView.m` to open the file.

3. Add the following `awakeFromNib` method:

```
- (void) awakeFromNib {
    [self setWantsLayer:YES];
}
```

4. In the `drawRect:` method, add the following code:

```
NSBezierPath *path = [NSBezierPath bezierPathWithRoundedRect:[self
    bounds] xRadius:8.0 yRadius:8.0];
[path setClip];

[[NSColor whiteColor] setFill];
[NSBezierPath fillRect:[self bounds]];

[path setLineWidth:3.0];

[[NSColor grayColor] setStroke];
[path stroke];
```

5. Click on `MediaTimingAppDelegate.h` to open it.

6. Add an import for the `MyView.h` header file:

```
#import "MyView.h"
```

7. We need to add two variables to the class interface:

```
NSButton *button;
MyView *myView;
```

8. Next we need to add property statements for each of the variables that we just added:

```
@property (assign) IBOutlet NSButton *button;
@property (assign) IBOutlet MyView *myView;
```

9. Lastly, add a method declaration for the button's action:

```
- (IBAction) animateButtonHit:(id)sender;
```

10. Click on `MediaTimingAppDelegate.m` to open the class implementation.

11. Add an import for `QuartzCore`:

    ```
    #import <QuartzCore/QuartzCore.h>
    ```

12. In the project view, expand the **Frameworks** group and then expand **Other Frameworks**. Right-click on **Other Frameworks** and choose **Add...**, then choose **Existing Frameworks...** Find **QuartzCore.framework** in the list of frameworks and choose **Add**.

13. We need to synthesize the button and `myView` variables:

    ```
    @synthesize button;
    @synthesize myView;
    ```

14. Lastly, lets add the `animateButtonHit:` methodit$ method" :

    ```
    - (IBAction) animateButtonHit:(id)sender {
      CABasicAnimation *animation = [CABasicAnimation
        animationWithKeyPath:@"opacity"];
      [animation setDuration:1.5];
      [animation setRepeatCount:1e100f];
      [animation setAutoreverses:YES];
      [animation setFromValue:[NSNumber numberWithFloat: 1.0]];
        [animation setToValue:[NSNumber numberWithFloat:0.1]];
      [animation setTimingFunction:[CAMediaTimingFunction
        functionWithName:kCAMediaTimingFunctionEaseInEaseOut]];
      [[myView layer] addAnimation:animation forKey:nil];
    }
    ```

15. Double-click on the `MainMenu.xib` file to open it in Interface Builder.

16. From the Library palette, drag a **Custom View** into the application window.

17. Select the **Identity** tab from the Inspector palette and set the **Class** popup to **MyView**.

18. Drag a **Push Button** from the Library palette to the application window. Set the button's title to **Animate**.

19. Next, we need to set the outlets and actions. In the `MainMenu.xib` project window, right-click on the **Media Timing App Delegate** to display the outlet connections window:

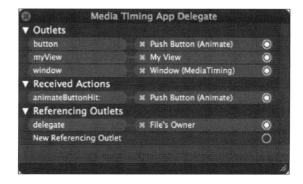

20. Next, drag a connection from the **myView** outlet to the **MyView Custom View**.

21. Finally, connect the **animateButtonHit:** action to the **Push Button**.

22. In Xcode, choose **Build and Run** from the toolbar to run the application.

How it works...

As we have done in other recipes, we create a custom view and call `setWantsLayer:YES` in the `awakeFromNib` method to enable the use of layers in the view.

In the `animateButtonHit:` method, we create a `CABasicAnimation` using the opacity key path with a duration of a second and a half. This animation will set the opacity property of the view's layer from 1.0 to 0.1. We set the animation to repeat forever using the value of 1e100f. Setting the auto reverse property to true will cause the animation to animate while setting the opacity property of the layer back to the original values.

Finally, we set the timing function property of the animation to the `kCAMediaTimingFunctionEaseInEaseOut` function. Using a media timing function will set the pace of the animation.

There's more...

In this recipe, we used the `kCAMediaTimingFunctionEaseInEaseOut` function for our animation. Even though there are other constants that you can use for the supplied functions, the `CAMediaTimingFunction` class allows you to define your own timing curve using the `functionWithControlPoints:` method.

See also

The sample code and project for this recipe is located under the `MediaTiming` folder in the code bundled with this book.

5

Objective-C 2.0

In this chapter, we will cover:

- ► Using blocks
- ► Switching compilers
- ► Create your own framework
- ► Using garbage collection
- ► Fast enumeration
- ► Declared properties

Introduction

In this chapter, we will use some of the new features available in the latest version of the Objective-C language. We will also show how to create a Framework project and use our Framework within an application.

Some of the new features of Objective-C we will cover will include using garbage collection, blocks, and switching to a more modern compiler. Be aware that using most of these features will limit backwards compatibility both in source and binary form.

 Some recipes in this chapter require Mac OS X Snow Leopard 10.6.

Using blocks

Blocks are a powerful new construct, which allow you to define a collection of code inline. Some other programming languages call blocks "closures". Usually, blocks represent small bits of code used to operate on a collection of items or as a callback method.

In this recipe, we will use blocks to iterate over the data in an NSArray. The NSArray class provides methods to which you can pass blocks to operate on the items within the array.

Getting ready

In Xcode, create a new Cocoa Application and name it Blocks.

How to do it...

1. In the Xcode project, click on the BlocksAppDelegate.m file to open it.
2. Add the following code in the applicationDidFinishLaunching: method:

```
NSArray *array = [NSArray arrayWithObjects:@"one", @"two",
    @"three", @"four", nil];

array = [array sortedArrayUsingComparator:
            ^(id a, id b)
            {
               if ([a isKindOfClass:[NSString class]] && [b
                 isKindOfClass:[NSString class]]) {
                 return [a compare:b
                   options:NSCaseInsensitiveSearch];
               }

               return (NSInteger) NSOrderedSame;
            }];


void (^printItem)(id obj, NSUInteger idx, BOOL *stop);

printItem = ^ (id obj, NSUInteger idx, BOOL *stop) {
  NSLog(@"Object: %@", obj);
};

[array enumerateObjectsUsingBlock:printItem];
```

3. Choose **Build and Run** from the Xcode toolbar to run the application.
4. View the console to see the output from running the application.

How it works...

First we create an NSArray with several values that we will later sort using a block. Using NSArray's sortedArraysUsingComparator method, which accepts a block for the comparison, we sort the array. The block is defined using the ^ character followed by the required parameters. In this case, the parameters are two ids, a and b. Since the block is defined using the type id rather than NSString, we used the isKindOfClass to ensure that the values passed to our block are of type NSString. We then use NSString's compare:options: method to actually compare the strings as this returns the required NSComparisonResult value.

Finally, we define a Block called printItem that will simply print each item that it sees to the console using NSLog. We pass our printItem block as an argument to the enumerateObjectsUsingBlock: method of the array so that we can print each item to the console.

There's more...

If you need to debug blocks, you can set breakpoints within them and step through the block's code as you normally would during debugging. You can also call blocks directly from within the debugger by using the *invoke-block* command.

See also

The sample code and project for this recipe is located under the Blocks folder in the code bundled with this book.

Switching compilers

This recipe will show you how to switch from the standard GCC compiler to the more modern Low Level Virtual Machine or LLVM Clang compiler that Apple now provides.

Getting ready

You may want to open one of your existing Xcode projects or open one of the sample projects from the code samples available with this book.

How to do it...

1. From the **Project** menu, choose **Edit Project Settings**.
2. Choose the **Build** tab.
3. From the **Configuration** popup, choose **All Configurations**.

4. In the search field type **Compiler Version**.

5. Set the value for the **C/C++ Compiler Version** to **LLVM compiler 1.5**:

How it works...

After editing the projects settings to use the LLVM compiler 1.5, you should clean your Xcode project and re-build.

There's more...

After you change from the compiler to use the newer LLVM/Clang compiler, you will notice that the project settings change. Several new sections appear where you can set two options for **LLVM compiler 1.5 – Code Generation**, **LLVM compiler 1.5 – Language**, **LLVM compiler 1.5 – Preprocessing**, and **LLVM compiler 1.5 – Warnings**.

See also

If you would like more information on the benefits of using the LLVM/Clang compiler you can find additional information at `http://llvm.org/`.

Create your own framework

In this recipe, we will create a framework and a sample application that uses the framework we created. Using a framework is a great way to package reusable functionality for use in your projects or for other developers projects.

Getting ready

In Xcode, create a new project. Under the **Mac OS X** section, choose **Framework and Library** and then choose the **Cocoa Framework** template. Name the new framework `MyFramework` and then save it:

How to do it...

1. In Xcode, expand the **Classes** group, right-click and choose **Add...**, then choose **New File...** Choose **Cocoa Class** from the **Mac OS X** section and select **Objective-C** class. In the **Subclass of** popup, choose **NSObject**. Name the file `MyClass` and then click on **Finish**.

2. Select `MyClass.h` from the Xcode project to open it.

3. Add the following method declaration:

   ```
   - (void)printName:(NSString *)name;
   ```

4. Select `MyClass.m` to open it.

5. Add the following method to the `MyClass` implementation:

```
- (void)printName:(NSString *)name {
    NSLog(@"Name: %@", name);
}
```

6. In the Xcode project, expand the **Targets** group and select `MyFramework`.

7. From the **Detail** view, change the **Role** popup from **project** to **public** for the `MyClass.h` file:

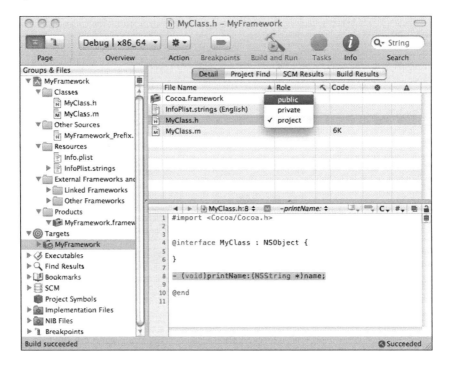

8. With **MyFramework** still selected under the **Targets** group, select **Get Info** from the **File** menu.

9. Select the **Build** tab and type **Installation Directory** in the search field.

10. Set the value of **Installation Directory** to **@executable_path/../Frameworks**.

11. From the **Build** menu, choose **Build** to build the framework.

12. Create a new Cocoa application and name it **MyApp**.

13. In the Xcode project, expand the **Frameworks** group and expand the **Linked Frameworks** group.

14. Right-click on the **Linked Frameworks** group and choose **Add...**, then choose **Existing Frameworks**. Click on the **Add Other...** button to navigate to the **MyFramework** framework we just created and choose **Add**.

15. Expand the **MyApp** group under the **Targets** group in the Xcode project.

16. Right-click on **MyApp** and choose **New Build Phase**, then choose **New Copy Files Build Phase**.

17. Select the new **Copy Files** phase and choose **Get Info** from the **File** menu.

18. In the **Get Info** window, select the **General** tab.

19. Set the **Destination** popup to **Frameworks** and close the window.

20. Next, drag the **MyFramework.framework** from the **Linked Frameworks** group to the new **Copy Files** phase that you just created.

21. Click on the `MyClass.m` to open it.

22. Add the following import line:

    `#import <MyFramework/MyClass.h>`

23. Use the following code for the `applicationDidFinishLaunching:` method:

    ```
    MyClass *myClass = [[[MyClass alloc] init] autorelease];
    [myClass printName:@"Packt Publishing"];
    ```

24. Choose **Build and Run** from the Xcode toolbar to run the application.

25. View the console to see the output from calling our framework.

How it works...

Using Xcode's Framework project template, we create a new framework and add the code that we want to use in the framework. We next set several settings on the framework's target so that it can be embedded properly into an application.

We set two settings on the frameworks target. The first is making the header file or files public as we did above in step 7. The second is setting the Installation Directory's path to `@executable_path/../Frameworks` so that the dynamic linker can locate the framework at runtime.

There's more...

In order for the Framework to be embedded correctly into the application that you are including the framework into, it is important to set the frameworks **Installation Directory** to @ executable_path/../Frameworks. The @executable_path is a special Xcode variable that will be substituted with the path to the executable in the applications bundle. By adding /../Frameworks, we are telling the dynamic linker where to look for our framework within the bundle. The following screenshot shows the contents of the MyApp bundle directory with the MyFramework included:

See also

The sample code and project for this recipe is located under the MyFramework and MyApp folder in the code bundled with this book.

Using garbage collection

Using garbage collection frees the developer from manual memory management. This recipe will show how to enable this feature in your Xcode projects.

Getting ready

You may want to open one of your existing Xcode projects or open one of the sample projects from the code samples available with this book.

How to do it...

1. From the **Project** menu, choose **Edit Project Settings**.
2. Choose the **Build** tab.
3. From the **Configuration** popup, choose **All Configurations**.
4. In the search field type **Garbage Collection**.
5. From the **Value** popup, select **Supported [-fobjc-gc]**:

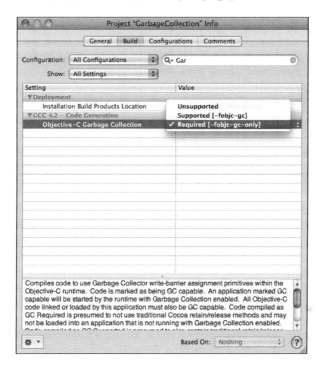

6. Close the project settings window.
7. From the **Build** menu, choose **Clean All Targets**.
8. Choose **Build and Run** from Xcode toolbar to run the application.

How it works...

By setting the `-fobjc-gc-only` compiler flag, you are building your code as garbage collection enabled. With this option set, you no longer need to manually manage object retain counts. This option is best used when starting new Cocoa projects for which you want to use garbage collection. You must be careful using this option, as you will not be able to use older frameworks whose memory is managed manually. Also note, the current version of iOS does not support the use of garbage collection.

Note that you may also use the -fobjc-gc compiler flag when you would like to use garbage collection with existing code that also manages memory using retain and release methods. This option is best used when your project makes use of third party libraries or code that manages memory manually.

There's more...

In some cases, it may be necessary to invoke the garbage collector manually to collect unused objects. You can call the NSGarbageCollector class collectIfNeeded method as follows:

```
NSGarbageCollector *garbageCollector = [NSGarbageCollector
    defaultCollector];
[garbageCollector collectIfNeeded];
```

See also

The sample code and project for this recipe is located under the GarbageCollection folder in the code bundled with this book.

Fast enumeration

In this recipe, we will use the new syntax for writing *for* loops. This new syntax is much more compact which results in less typing. We will also cover which collection types can be used with fast enumeration.

Getting ready

In Xcode, create a new Cocoa Application and name it FastEnumeration.

How to do it...

1. Click on FastEnumerationAppDelegate.m to open it.

2. In the applicationDidFinishLaunching: method, add the following code:

```
NSArray *array = [NSArray arrayWithObjects:@"object 1", @"object
    2", @"object 3", @"object 4", @"object 5", nil];

for (NSString *object in array) {
  NSLog(@"Object: %@", object);
}

for (NSString *object in [array reverseObjectEnumerator]) {
  NSLog(@"Object: %@", object);
}
```

3. Click **Build and Run** from Xcode's toolbar to run the application.

4. View the console to see the output from running the application.

How it works...

Fast enumeration is supported by a new syntax to define the *for* loop. Basically, you define a variable of the same type used in the collection within the *for* loop followed by the keyword *in*, followed by an expression.

`NSArray`, `NSDictionary`, `NSSet`, and `NSEnumeration` adopt the `NSFastEnumeration` protocol and therefore can be used with the new *for* loop syntax. You can also use the `reverseObjectEnumerator` method of the `NSArray` class to loop through the array in reverse.

There's more...

By adopting the `NSFastEnumeration` protocol in your own classes, you can support the fast enumeration syntax with your own classes.

See also

The sample code and project for this recipe is located under the `FastEnumeration` folder in the code bundled with this book.

Declared properties

Declared properties are a new way to specify getters and setters for your class variables. It requires much less typing as the compiler generates the methods for you based on the attributes you specify.

In this recipe, we will declare a few variables using properties. Using specific attributes, we will change the name of the getters and setters that will be automatically generated for us.

Getting ready

In Xcode, create a new Cocoa Application and name it `Properties`.

How to do it...

1. Click on `PropertiesAppDelegate.h` to open it.

2. Add the following two variables to the class interface:

```
BOOL running;
NSString *name;
```

3. Next, add a property for each of the variables that we just added below the property for the window variable:

```
@property (assign, getter=isRunning, setter=startRunning) BOOL
    running;
@property (retain) NSString *name;
```

4. Click on `PropertiesAppDelegate.m` to open it.

5. Below the `synthesize` directive for the window variable, add the following `synthesize` directive for our two new variables:

```
@synthesize running, name;
```

6. Next, add the following code in the `applicationDidFinishLaunching:` method:

```
[self startRunning:YES];

NSLog(@"isRunning: %d", [self isRunning]);

[self setName:@"Packt"];
NSLog(@"name: %@", [self name]);

NSLog(@"isRunning: %d", self.isRunning);
NSLog(@"name: %@", self.name);
```

7. Choose **Build and Run** from Xcode's toolbar to run the application.

8. View the console to see the output from the application.

How it works...

We first declare a few variables as we normally would in the class interface. We then use the `@property` keyword with each variable and list a few attributes, which will determine how our getters and setters will be created. The assign attribute indicates that we will be making a simple assignment in the setter. The `getter=isRunning` attribute sets the name of the getter method, while the `setter=startRunning` attribute sets the name of the setter method. Note that you still need to use the type of variable and the variable name at the end of the property declaration.

The @property of the name variable uses the retain attribute. This tells the compiler to generate a setter that will call retain on the name being set and release on the previous name. Much like you would do when writing your own setter methods.

Lastly, note how we used the new dotted notation to access the isRunning and name properties in the last two NSLog statements. This is also a new feature in Objective-C 2.0 that reduces the use of square brackets and makes the syntax similar to other more popular languages.

There's more...

There is another attribute that can be used when declaring properties called nonatomic. This attribute specifies that the getter returns the value directly without regard for use in a multi-threaded environment.

Note that there is no atomic attribute and getters are atomic by default, which allows them to be used safely in a multi-threaded environment.

See also

The sample code and project for this recipe is located under the Properties folder in the code bundled with this book.

6
Application Architecture

In this chapter, we will cover:

- ▸ The Singleton design pattern
- ▸ The Factory design pattern
- ▸ Using delegation in your own classes
- ▸ Using an NSTimer for periodic events
- ▸ Working with Key-Value Coding
- ▸ Using operators with Key Value Paths
- ▸ Using NSAutoreleasePool

Introduction

In this chapters, recipes we will cover some basic architecture topics. The common design patterns we will discuss will help you build applications that are more maintainable and structured. We will also show how you can leverage Key-Value Coding and use operators with Key Value Paths to simplify your classes.

The Singleton design pattern

The singleton design pattern is used when you need one and only one object created during the lifetime of your application. In this recipe, you will create a singleton class that contains a name property.

In this recipe, we will not create a Cocoa application but rather just demonstrate how the class interface and implementation should be defined.

How to do it...

1. The singleton's interface is defined as follows:

```
#import <Cocoa/Cocoa.h>


@interface Context : NSObject {
  NSString *name;
}

@property (retain) NSString *name;


+ (Context *)sharedInstance;

@end
```

2. The singleton's implementation is defined as follows:

```
#import "Context.h"


@implementation Context

@synthesize name;


static Context *sharedInstance = nil;

+ (Context *)sharedInstance
{
    if (sharedInstance == nil) {
        sharedInstance = [[super allocWithZone:NULL] init];
    }

    return sharedInstance;
}
```

```objc
+ (id)allocWithZone:(NSZone *)zone
{
    return [self sharedInstance];
}

- (id)copyWithZone:(NSZone *)zone
{
    return self;
}

- (id)retain
{
    return self;
}

- (NSUInteger)retainCount
{
    return NSUIntegerMax;
}

- (void)release
{
}

- (id)autorelease
{
    return self;
}

@end
```

How it works...

In the class's interface, we define the class method, `sharedInstance`, which will provide us with a reference to our class. In the `sharedInstance` method, we check to see if the `sharedInstance` static variable is nil and if so allocate, initialize, and return our singleton class. This ensures that only one instance of this class will be created. We override the `allocWithZone:` method to return the singleton instance. This prevents users from directly allocating and initializing an instance of our class.

Finally, we override `retain`, `retainCount`, `release`, and `autorelease` to prevent the disposing of our class.

The sample code and project for this recipe is located under the `Singleton` folder in the code bundled with this book.

The Factory design pattern

In this recipe, we will create a class that implements the factory design pattern. The factory design pattern is used to create objects which might be difficult to create or set up.

Getting ready

In this recipe, we will not create a Cocoa application but rather just demonstrate how the class interface and implementation should be defined. Our factory will create different types of `CAAnimation`'s for use with a `CALayer`.

How to do it...

1. The factory interface is defined as follows:

```
#import <Cocoa/Cocoa.h>
#import <QuartzCore/QuartzCore.h>

@interface AnimationFactory : NSObject {

}

+ (CAAnimation *) createOpacityAnimation;
+ (CAAnimation *) createScaleAnimation;
+ (CAAnimation *) createRotationAnimation;

@end
```

2. The factory implementation is defined as follows:

```
#import "AnimationFactory.h"


@implementation AnimationFactory

+ (CAAnimation *) createOpacityAnimation {
  CABasicAnimation *fadeAnimation = [CABasicAnimation
    animationWithKeyPath:@"opacity"];
  [fadeAnimation setAutoreverses:YES];
```

```
    [fadeAnimation setToValue:[NSNumber numberWithFloat:0.0]];

    return fadeAnimation;
}

+ (CAAnimation *) createScaleAnimation {
    CABasicAnimation *scaleAnimation = [CABasicAnimation
      animationWithKeyPath:@"transform.scale"];
    [scaleAnimation setAutoreverses:YES];
    [scaleAnimation setToValue:[NSNumber numberWithFloat:0.0]];

    return scaleAnimation;
}

+ (CAAnimation *) createRotationAnimation {
    CATransform3D transform = CATransform3DMakeRotation(M_PI, 0.0f,
      1.0f, 0.0f);
    CABasicAnimation *rotateAnimation = [CABasicAnimation
      animationWithKeyPath:@"transform.rotation"];
    [rotateAnimation setToValue:[NSValue
      valueWithCATransform3D:transform]];

    return rotateAnimation;
}

@end
```

How it works...

Our factory class implements three class methods that create, configure, and return a `CAAnimation` reference. Each method creates a `CABasicAnimation` with a specific key path and configures the animation with various properties before returning the animation.

See also

The sample code and project for this recipe is located under the `Factory` folder in the code bundled with this book.

Using delegation in your own classes

In this recipe, we will show how to use a delegate in your own classes. Using delegation allows you to let other classes provide functionality in your class by calling out to the delegate.

Getting ready

In Xcode, create a new Cocoa Application and name it `Delegation`.

How to do it...

1. Add a new protocol to the project and name it `DeleteNameProtocol.h`:

2. Select `DeleteNameProtocol.h` to open it and add the following method declaration:

    ```
    - (BOOL) shouldDeleteName:(NSString *)name;
    ```

3. Add a new class to the project and name it `MyNames`.

4. Click on `MyNames.h` to open it.

5. Add the import for the protocol:

    ```
    #import "DeleteNameProtocol.h"
    ```

6. Add the two variables below to the class interface:

    ```
    NSMutableArray *array;
    id<DeleteNameProtocol, NSObject> delegate;
    ```

7. Next add the following properties:

```
@property (retain) NSMutableArray *array;
@property (assign) id<DeleteNameProtocol, NSObject> delegate;
```

8. Add a declaration for the `deleteName:` method:

```
- (void) deleteName:(NSString *)name;
```

9. Open `MyNames.m` and synthesize the two variables that we added to the interface:

```
@synthesize array;
@synthesize delegate;
```

10. Add the following methods to the class implementation:

```
- (id) init {
  self = [super init];
  if (self != nil) {
    array = [[NSMutableArray alloc] init];
    [array addObject:@"Packt Publishing"];
    [array addObject:@"Ben"];
    [array addObject:@"Jeffrey"];
    [array addObject:@"George"];
    [array addObject:@"Thomas"];
  }

  return self;
}

- (void) deleteName:(NSString *)name {
  if ([array containsObject:name] == YES) {
    if (delegate != nil) {
      if ([delegate  respondsToSelector:@selector(shouldDeleteName
:)]
        == YES) {
        if ([delegate shouldDeleteName:name] == YES) {
          [array removeObject:name];
        }
      }
    }
  }
}

- (void) dealloc {
  [array release];

  [super dealloc];
}
```

11. Click on the `DelegationAppDelegate.h` file to open it.

12. Add the import for the protocol:

```
#import "DeleteNameProtocol.h"
```

13. Add the protocol to the class interface:

```
<NSApplicationDelegate, DeleteNameProtocol>
```

14. Open the `DelegationAppDelegate.m`

15. Add an import for the `MyNames` class:

```
#import "MyNames.h"
```

16. Next, add the following to the `applicationDidFinishLaunching:` method:

```
MyNames *names = [[[MyNames alloc] init] autorelease];
[names setDelegate:self];

[names deleteName:@"Jeffrey"];
```

17. Finally, add the `shouldDeleteName:` method:

```
- (BOOL) shouldDeleteName:(NSString *)name {
  if (name isEqualToString:@"Jeffrey"] == YES) {
    NSLog(@"Deleting Name: %@", name);
    return YES;
  }

  return NO;
}
```

18. Choose **Build and Run** from the toolbar to run the application:

```
[Switching to process 1447]
Running...
2011-04-06 23:03:30.056 Delegation[1447:a0f] Deleting Name: Jeffrey
```

How it works...

First we create a Protocol that describes the methods that we need the delegate to implement. In our sample we are asking the delegate to implement the `shouldDeleteName:` method. When the user of our class calls the `deleteName:` method, we check that the delegate has been set and call `respondsToSelector:` to determine if the delegate has implemented our protocol method. If they have implemented the protocols method, we call the `shouldDeleteName:` method on the delegates class and if it returns `YES`, we delete the name from our array.

There's more...

Our class contains an id<DeleteNameProtocol, NSObject> variable for the delegate. When we define the delegate variable using the @property keyword, we need to use the assign attribute since we want a weak reference to the delegate.

You can verify that a class conforms to a specified protocol at runtime by using the conformsToProtocol: method provided by the NSObject class.

See also

The sample code and project for this recipe is located under the Delegation folder in the code bundled with this book.

Using an NSTimer for periodic events

In this recipe, we will create an NSTimer to call a method every three seconds. We will build a simple interface with two buttons, one to start the timer and one to stop the timer.

Getting ready

In Xcode, create a new Cocoa Application and name it NSTimer.

How to do it...

1. Open the NSTimerAppDelegate.h file.

2. Add the following variables to the class interface:

    ```
    NSButton *start;
    NSButton *stop;
    NSTimer *timer;
    ```

3. Add properties for each of the above variables:

    ```
    @property (assign) NSButton *start;
    @property (assign) NSButton *stop;
    @property (assign) NSTimer *timer;
    ```

4. Next add the following method declarations:

    ```
    - (IBAction) startTimer:(id)sender;
    - (IBAction) stopTimer:(id)sender;
    ```

5. Click on the NSTimerAppDelegate.m to open it.

6. Synthesize the variables that we added in the class interface:

```
@synthesize start;
@synthesize stop;
@synthesize timer;
```

7. Add the following methods to finish the class implementation:

```
(IBAction) startTimer:(id)sender {
if (timer != nil) {
    [timer invalidate];
   }

    timer = [NSTimer scheduledTimerWithTimeInterval:3 target:self
      selector:@selector(timerFired:) userInfo:nil repeats:YES];
}

-  (IBAction) stopTimer:(id)sender {
   [timer invalidate];
   timer = nil;
}

-  (void) timerFired:(NSTimer *)timer {
   NSLog(@"Timer Fired: %@", [[NSDate date] description]);
}
```

8. Double click the `MainMenu.xib` file in the Xcode project to open it in Interface Builder.

9. From the Library pallet in Interface Builder, drag two **Push Buttons** to the application window. Your application window should look like the following screenshot:

10. Set the title for the first Push Button to **Start**.

11. Set the title for the second Push Button to **Stop**.

12. Next, right-click on the **Timer App Delegate** so that we can connect the outlets and actions:

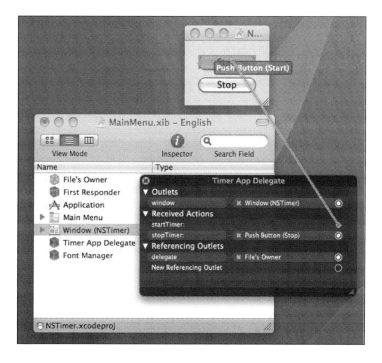

13. Back in Xcode, choose **Build and Run** from the toolbar.

14. View the console to see the results while the application is running.

How it works...

Creating an NSTimer is pretty straightforward. The NSTimer class provides several class methods that can be used to configure and return a timer. In our example, we create a timer that will fire every three seconds. When the timer fires, it will call our class's timerFired: method. Notice that we use the @selector() syntax tell the timer which method to call when firing the timer. Although we pass nil for the userInfo: parameter, you may supply an NSDictionary or other class, with values to be passed to the timerFired: method.

See also

The sample code and project for this recipe is located under the NSTimer folder in the code bundled with this book.

Working with Key-Value Coding

Key-Value Coding is a technology that allows applications to set and retrieve class properties by name. In this recipe, we will create a class property and update that property using Key-Value Coding.

Getting ready

In Xcode, create a new Cocoa Application and name it `KeyValueCoding`.

How to do it...

1. Click on the `KeyValueCodingAppDelegate.h` file to open the class interface.

2. Add the following variables to the class:

   ```
   NSInteger count;
   NSButton *button;
   ```

3. Next, add properties for each of the variables we added:

   ```
   @property (assign) NSInteger count;
   @property (retain) NSButton *button;
   ```

4. Add a method declaration for the button's action:

   ```
   - (IBAction) buttonHit:(id)sender;
   ```

5. Click on the `KeyValueCodingAppDelegate.m` to open the class implementation file.

6. Synthesize the variables we added to the class:

   ```
   @synthesize count;
   @synthesize button;
   ```

7. Add the button's action method to the class implementation:

   ```
   - (IBAction) buttonHit:(id)sender {
     for (NSInteger i = 0; i < 10000; i++) {
       [self setValue:[NSNumber numberWithInt:i] forKey:@"count"];
     }
   }
   ```

8. Double-click on `MainMenu.xib` to open the Interface Builder.

9. Drag a **Push Button**, **Label**, and a **Text Field** from the library pallete into the applications window. The layout should look similar to the following:

10. Right-click on the **Key Value App Delegate** to open the outlets window so that we can connect our button action:

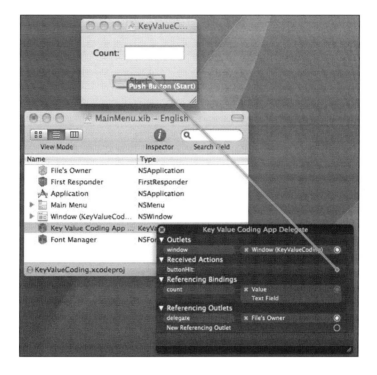

11. Next, we need to bind our Text Field to the count variable. Select the Text Field and choose the **Bindings** tab of the Inspector pallete.

12. Select the **Bind to:** checkbox and select **Key Value App Delegate** from the popup.

13. In the **Model Key Path** combobox, type count. Your binding should look like the following screenshot:

14. Back in Xcode, choose **Build and Run** from the toolbar to run the application.

How it works...

The sample code demonstrates that we can update the count variable by calling the `setValue:forKey` method rather than calling the `setCount:` method directly. This works by calling our variables setter method, `setCount:`, which was created for us when we used the `@property` and `@synthesize` keywords. In order for Key-Value Coding to work properly, it is important that the methods used to set and access your variables follow Apple's naming conventions. You can find more information about naming conventions in regards to Key-Value Coding in Apple's *Key-Value Programming Guide*. You can find the *Key-Value Programing Guide* online at the following link: `http://developer.apple.com/library/mac/#documentation/Cocoa/Conceptual/KeyValueCoding/Articles/KeyValueCoding.html`.

There's more...

To ensure that your class works effectively with Key-Value Coding, you should implement the `-(void)setNilValueForKey:(NSString *)theKey` method to properly handle the case where your class receives a nil value when called from the `setValue:forKey:` method.

See also

The sample code and project for this recipe is located under the `KeyValueCoding` folder in the code bundled with this book.

Using operators with Key Value Paths

Collection operators allow you to perform operations on a collection of objects using key paths. In this recipe, we will show you how to use the five most common operators.

Getting ready

In Xcode, create a new Cocoa Application and name it `Operators`.

How to do it...

1. Right-click on the **Classes** group in the Xcode project view and choose **Add...** then choose **New File...**

2. In the **New File** window, choose **Cocoa Class** from the **Mac OS X** section and then choose **Objective-C class**. In the **Subclass of** popup, select **NSObject** and click on **Next** and name the class **Widget**:

3. Click on the `Widget.h` file to open it and add a `width` variable to the class:

   ```
   NSInteger width;
   ```

4. Add a property for the width variable:

```
@property (assign) NSInteger width;
```

5. Click on the `Widget.m` file to open the class implementation.

6. Synthesize the `width` variable:

```
@synthesize width;
```

7. Click on `OperatorsAppDelegate.h` to open the file.

8. Add a `NSMutableArray` variable to the class interface:

```
NSMutableArray *array;
```

9. Click on the `OperatorsAppDelegate.m` file to open it.

10. Add an import for the `Widget.h` file:

```
#import "Widget.h"
```

11. Finally, add the following code to the `applicationDidFinishLaunching:` method:

```
array = [[NSMutableArray alloc] init];
Widget *widget = [[[Widget alloc] init] autorelease];
[widget setWidth:10];
[array addObject:widget];

widget = [[[Widget alloc] init] autorelease];
[widget setWidth:20];
[array addObject:widget];

widget = [[[Widget alloc] init] autorelease];
[widget setWidth:20];
[array addObject:widget];

widget = [[[Widget alloc] init] autorelease];
[widget setWidth:40];
[array addObject:widget];

NSNumber *value = [array valueForKeyPath:@"@count"];
NSLog(@"Count: %f", [value doubleValue]);

value = [array valueForKeyPath:@"@max.width"];
NSLog(@"Max: %f", [value doubleValue]);

value = [array valueForKeyPath:@"@min.width"];
NSLog(@"Min: %f", [value doubleValue]);

value = [array valueForKeyPath:@"@sum.width"];
NSLog(@"Sum: %f", [value doubleValue]);
```

12. Choose **Build and Run** from the toolbar to run the application.

13. View the console to see the results:

```
[Switching to process 1358]
Running…
2011-04-06 22:50:55.256 Operators[1358:a0f] Count: 4.000000
2011-04-06 22:50:55.258 Operators[1358:a0f] Max: 40.000000
2011-04-06 22:50:55.259 Operators[1358:a0f] Min: 10.000000
2011-04-06 22:50:55.259 Operators[1358:a0f] Sum: 90.000000
```

How it works...

In this example, we create a simple class named `Widget` that contains a `width` property, which we will access with via a key path. We then add several widgets to an array.

Using the `valueForKeyPath:` method on the array class, we can find the number of objects in the array using the `@count` key path. Note that the value returned is not an `NSUInteger`, but rather an `NSNumber` object.

Using key paths, you can perform other operations on the array of objects as well. We use the `@max.width` key path to find the widget's largest width in the array. We can find the smallest width using the `@min.width` key path. Lastly, we can find the sum of all the widgets width using the `@sum.width` key path.

There's more...

There are other operators available when using arrays or sets that contain other arrays. Operators such as `@distinctUnionOfArrays` and `@unionOfArrays` can be used on these collections and return their results as a new NSArray.

See also

The sample code and project for this recipe is located under the `Operators` folder in the code bundled with this book.

Using NSAutoreleasePool

In this recipe, we will demonstrate how to use an `NSAutoreleasePool` effectively. If your application allocates many autoreleased objects, especially within *for* or *while* loops, you will want to use an `NSAutoreleasePool` to better manage the memory footprint of the application.

Getting ready

In Xcode, create a new Cocoa Application and name it NSAutoreleasePool.

How to do it...

1. Click on NSAutoreleasePoolAppDelegate.h to open the class interface.

2. Add the variables below to the class:

    ```
    NSButton *buttonOne;
    NSButton *buttonTwo;
    ```

3. Add properties for the variables to the class as follows:

    ```
    @property (retain) IBOutlet NSButton *buttonOne;
    @property (retain) IBOutlet NSButton *buttonTwo;
    ```

4. Add the two method declarations for our button actions:

    ```
    - (IBAction) buttonHit:(id)sender;
    - (IBAction) poolButtonHit:(id)sender;
    ```

5. Click on the NSAutoreleasePoolAppDelegate.m to open the class implementation.

6. Synthesize the variables we added to the class interface:

    ```
    @synthesize buttonOne;
    @synthesize buttonTwo;
    ```

7. Next, add the following button action methods to our class:

    ```
    - (IBAction) buttonHit:(id)sender {
      for (int i = 0; i < 100000; i++) {
        NSMutableString *string = [NSMutableString
          stringWithCapacity:100000];
      }
    }

    - (IBAction) poolButtonHit:(id)sender {
      for (int i = 0; i < 100000; i++) {
        NSAutoreleasePool *pool = [[NSAutoreleasePool alloc] init];
        NSMutableString *string = [NSMutableString
          stringWithCapacity:100000];
        [pool drain];
      }
    }
    ```

8. Double-click on MainMenu.xib to open it in Interface Builder.

9. Drag two **Push Buttons** and two **Labels** from the Library pallete to the application window. The layout should be similar to the following screenshot:

10. Right-click on the **Autorelease App Delegate** to open the outlet connections window so that we can connect our button's actions:

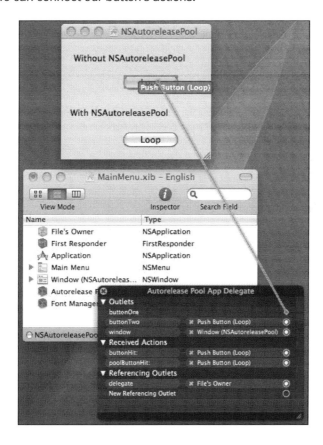

11. Back in Xcode, choose **Run**, then choose **Run with Performance Tool** and then choose **Leaks**.

How it works...

We have created two identical *for* loops that allocate a large number of mutable strings. The only difference between the two loops is the use of an `NSAutoreleasePool`. In the screenshots below, notice the difference in the **Overall Bytes** for the **CFString**:

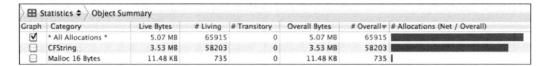

Leaks result without the use of `NSAutoreleasePool`.

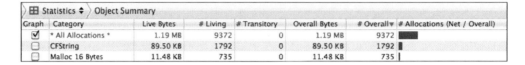

Leaks result when using `NSAutoreleasePool` in loop.

There's more...

If you are creating or detaching your own threads, you will want to create an `NSAutoreleasePool` within your thread as soon as possible to manage any autoreleased objects and prevent memory leaks. It is not necessary to drain the autorelease pool within a thread. When the thread exits, it will automatically drain the autorelease pool.

See also

The sample code and project for this recipe is located under the `NSAutoreleasePool` folder in the code bundled with this book.

7
Better Debugging

In this chapter, we will cover:

- ▶ Using special environment variables
- ▶ Using Instruments for performance
- ▶ Handling exceptions
- ▶ Knowing when you are being debugged
- ▶ Using Debugger() and DebugStr()
- ▶ Using Build and Analyze in Xcode

Introduction

In this chapter, we will look at several recipes that will help you build better applications by introducing tools to help debug issues. A large part of building successful applications is the debugging process. Any tools that can help you easily find and resolve issues with your application make the development process much more enjoyable. This chapter will introduce several tools and tips to help debug issues within your application.

Using special environment variables

In this recipe, we will take a look at several environment variables and preferences that can be set to help debug various issues in your applications.

Getting ready

Although you can set environment variables and preferences on the command line using the Terminal.app and run your application, it is much easier to set these within Xcode. By doing so, they will be enabled when you debug your application in Xcode.

How to do it...

1. Open an existing project in Xcode.

2. In the Xcode project view, expand the **Executables** group and right-click on the executable and choose **Get Info**.

3. Within the **Info** dialog, select the **Arguments** tab and you can add and remove environment variables and preferences (or Arguments) as needed.

4. Close the **Info** dialog.

5. Choose **Build and Run** from the toolbar to run the application:

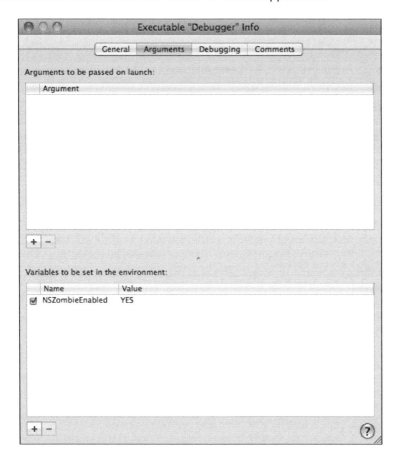

How it works...

The following lists some of the environment variables and preferences that can be used for additional debugging without having to modify any application code at all.

Environment Variables:

`MallocScribble` – When set to 1, fills all allocated memory with `0xAA` and all de-allocated memory with `0x55`.

`MallocGuardEdges` – Set to 1 to wrap large allocations with guard pages.

`NSObjCMessageLoggingEnabled` – Set to YES to log all Objective-C messages to the file `/tmp/msgSends-<pid>` where `<pid>` is the process id of your application.

`NSZombieEnabled` – When set to `YES`, a message will be logged on the console whenever you release a previously released object.

Preferences:

`NSShowAllViews` – Set to `YES` to have the `AppKit` draw an outline around all views.

`NSDebugFocusRing` – When set to `YES`, `AppKit` will highlight focus rings and log information to the console regarding the focus ring.

`NSTraceEvents` – Set to `YES` to have `AppKit` log all events to the console.

There's more...

Preferences can be set via the command line using `Terminal.app` using the *defaults* command. As an example, the command below will turn on the preference for showing all the views in the TextEdit application. After running the following, launch the TextEdit application, and you will see the colored outlines of all the views that make up the TextEdit document window.

```
defaults write com.apple.TextEdit NSShowAllViews YES
```

For more information on using the *defaults* command, see the *defaults* man page.

See also

Apple has created a technical note devoted to "secret" debugging techniques that can be used to find various issues within your application. You can find this technical note at the following location on the web:

`http://developer.apple.com/library/mac/#technotes/tn2004/tn2124.html`

Using Instruments for performance

In this recipe, we will look at the Instruments application provided with Xcode. The Instruments application can be used to track memory issues and performance problems within your application.

Getting ready

Instruments can be launched from within Xcode by choosing the **Run** menu and then choosing **Run with Performance Tool**.

If you want to run Instruments outside of Xcode, you can find it in the `Applications` folder within the `Developer` folder of your Xcode installation.

How to do it...

1. In Xcode, select the **Run** menu, then select **Run with Performance Tool** and choose a performance tool that you want to use. Most likely, you will want to use the Leaks tool to track down memory leaks.

2. Instruments will launch and start your application and begin sampling information from your application.

3. When you have collected enough information, click on the **Stop** button.

4. Without exiting Instruments, go back to Xcode and make any changes and rebuild your application.

5. You can return to Instruments and resample your application and Instruments will record the run. Note that Instruments will save each run so that you can compare differences between runs:

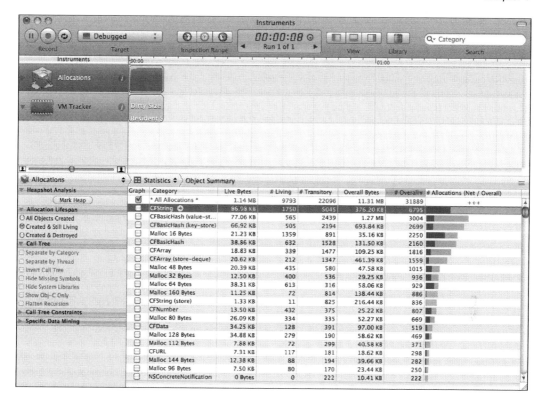

How it works

When you launch your application using Instruments, it takes samples of the internal state of your application at constant intervals. Since we are using the Allocations instrument we can view the memory allocations of all objects within our sample application. Note that you can use the search field to filter which class you want to watch. If we suspect that an object is not being released when it should be, we could use the information in Instruments and make changes in our code and rerun Instruments to see if we have corrected the issue. Since you can save and compare the runs within Instruments, you can verify if your fix did correct the allocation issue.

There's more...

Instruments allows you to build your own instrumentation using DTrace scripts. If you are interested in creating your own instruments, please refer to the section *Creating Custom Instruments with DTrace* in the Instruments User Guide.

The Instruments application has many features and can be intimidating when first learning how to use it effectively. You can find the Instruments user guide at the following location on the web:

```
http://developer.apple.com/library/mac/#DOCUMENTATION/DeveloperTools/
Conceptual/InstrumentsUserGuide/Introduction/Introduction.html.
```

Handling exceptions

Handling exceptions in Objective-C is very similar to other languages In this recipe, we will show how to use exceptions in Objective-C and how to use the NSExceptionHandler to aid logging exceptions in your applications.

Getting ready

In Xcode, create a new Cocoa Application project and name it Exceptions.

How to do it...

1. Click on ExecptionsAppDelegate.m to open it.

2. Add an import for NSExceptionHandler:

   ```
   #import <ExceptionHandling/NSExceptionHandler.h>
   ```

3. Right-click on **Frameworks** in the Xcode project view to expand it, then right-click on **Other Frameworks** and choose **Add**, then choose **Existing Frameworks**.... Select **ExceptionHandling.framework** and click on **Add**:

4. Add the following code to the `applicationDidFinishLaunching:` method:

```
[[NSExceptionHandler defaultExceptionHandler] setDelegate:self];
[[NSExceptionHandler defaultExceptionHandler]
  setExceptionHandlingMask: NSLogAndHandleEveryExceptionMask];

@try {

  if (YES) { // Change to NO and note finally is still called!!
    @throw [NSException exceptionWithName:@"BadException"
      reason:@"Illegal State Detected" userInfo:nil];
  }
}
@catch (NSException *e) {
  [[NSApplication sharedApplication] reportException:e];
}
@finally {
  NSLog(@"Finally called");
}
```

5. Finally, add the delegate method for the `NSExceptionHandler`:

```
- (BOOL)exceptionHandler:(NSExceptionHandler *)sender shouldLogExc
eption:(NSException *)exception mask:(NSUInteger)aMask {
  return YES;
}
```

6. Choose **Build and Run** from Xcode's toolbar to run the application. View the console to see the output of the application:

```
2011-04-10 19:45:18.642 Exceptions[3344:a0f] NSExceptionHandler has recorded the
following exception:
BadException -- Illegal State Detected
Stack trace:  0x7fff81386a2c  0x7fff8352d0f3  0x1000015b7  0x7fff850648ea
0x7fff859d5000  0x7fff859c1578  0x7fff8505b84e  0x7fff825433d6  0x7fff8254330b
0x7fff8260e305  0x7fff8260df81  0x7fff85092e42  0x7fff85092c72  0x7fff886cc323
0x7fff886cc21c  0x7fff886cc123  0x7fff8874e619  0x7fff8251304b  0x7fff825127a9
0x7fff824d848b  0x7fff824d11a8  0x100001515  0x1000014ec  0x1
2011-04-10 19:45:18.644 Exceptions[3344:a0f] Illegal State Detected
2011-04-10 19:45:18.645 Exceptions[3344:a0f] Finally called
```

How it works...

Exceptions in Objective-C are defined by using the following directives `@try`, `@catch`, `@throw`, and `@finally`. Any code that might throw an exception is wrapped in a `@try` block. If an exception is thrown, the `@catch` block is executed. The optional `@finally` block, if defined, will always be executed whether or not an exception is thrown.

The `NSExceptionHandler` handler class allows you to set delegates which will be notified of various exceptions depending on the mask value passed when calling the `setExceptionHandlingMask:` method on the default exception handler. When the delegates are called, you simply return YES or NO as to whether or not you want the exception logged. You can query the passed `NSException` to help determine which value to return from the delegate.

In order to use the `NSExceptionHandler` class, you must add the `ExceptionHandling` framework to your project. Note that if you are just using exceptions or handling exceptions within your application, you do not need to include this framework.

There's more...

You can use the `@throw` directive to throw any type of Objective-C object. You are not limited to throwing just `NSException` and any derived classes.

Although set by default, make sure you have enabled Objective-C exceptions in the project settings:

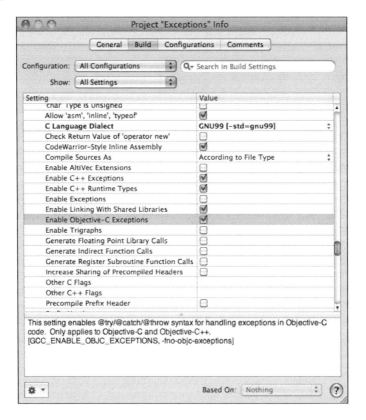

See also

The sample code and project for this recipe is located under the `Exceptions` folder in the code bundled with this book.

Knowing when you are being debugged

In this recipe, we will use some code from Apple to determine when your application is being run under the debugger. This may be useful if you need to print extra information to the console when running under the debugger or even prevent your application from being run at all when launched under a debugger.

Getting ready

In Xcode, create a new Cocoa Application project and name it `Debugged`.

How to do it...

1. Click on `DebuggedAppDelegate.h` to open it.

2. Add a method declaration for our class method:

   ```
   + (BOOL) AmIBeingDebugged
   ```

3. Click on `DebuggedAppDelegate.m` to open it.

4. Add the following include directives:

   ```
   #include <assert.h>
   #include <stdbool.h>
   #include <sys/types.h>
   #include <unistd.h>
   #include <sys/sysctl.h>
   ```

5. In the `applicationDidFinishLaunching:` method, add the following code:

   ```
   if ([DebuggedAppDelegate AmIBeingDebugged] == YES) {
      NSLog(@"I am being debugged.");
    } else {
      NSLog(@"I am NOT being debugged.");
   }
   ```

6. Add the following code that we copied from Apple's technical note into the body of the `AmIBeingDebugged()` method:

```
int            junk;
int            mib[4];
struct kinfo_proc   info;
size_t         size;

// Initialize the flags so that, if sysctl fails for some bizarre
// reason, we get a predictable result.

info.kp_proc.p_flag = 0;

// Initialize mib, which tells sysctl the info we want. In this
// case we're looking for information about a specific process ID.

mib[0] = CTL_KERN;
mib[1] = KERN_PROC;
mib[2] = KERN_PROC_PID;
mib[3] = getpid();

// Call sysctl.

size = sizeof(info);
junk = sysctl(mib, sizeof(mib) / sizeof(*mib), &info, &size, NULL,
   0);
assert(junk == 0);

// We're being debugged if the P_TRACED flag is set.

return ( (info.kp_proc.p_flag & P_TRACED) != 0 );
```

7. Choose **Build and Run** from the toolbar to run the application.

How it works...

When you run this application within Xcode, whether debugging or not, you will see **I am being debugged.** on the console. In order to test the case where the application detects that you are not being debugged, start the application from the Finder and view the output in the `Console.app`.

There's more...

The code for the `AmIBeingDebugged` method is available in the following technical note from Apple. Note that I have modified it slightly to make it a class method:

`http://developer.apple.com/library/mac/#qa/qa2004/qa1361.html`.

See also

The sample code and project for this recipe is located under the `Debugged` folder in the code bundled with this book.

Using Debugger() and DebugStr()

In this recipe, we will look at two functions that you can use to immediately break into the debugger when running your application.

Getting ready

In Xcode, create a new Cocoa Application project and name it `Debugger`.

How to do it...

1. Click on the `DebuggerAppDelegate.h` file so that we can add a property for the `NSButton` to the class interface:

    `@property (assign) IBOutlet NSButton *button;`

2. Add a method declaration for the method that will be called when the button is clicked:

    `- (IBAction) buttonHit:(id)sender;`

3. Click on the `DebuggerAppDelegate.m` file to open it.

4. Synthesize the button variable:

    `@synthesize button;`

5. Add the following `buttonHit:` method:

```
- (IBAction) buttonHit:(id)sender {
  for (NSInteger i = 0; i < 500; i++) {

    if (i == 200) {
      Debugger();
    } else if (i == 250) {
      DebugStr("\pHere we are");
    }
  }
}
```

6. Double-click the `MainMenu.xib` file to open it in Interface Builder.

7. From the Library pallete in Interface Builder, drag a **Push Button** to the application window.

8. Set the button's title to **Debugger**.

9. Connect the button's outlets and actions by right-clicking on the **Debugger App Delegate** from the MainMenu's window:

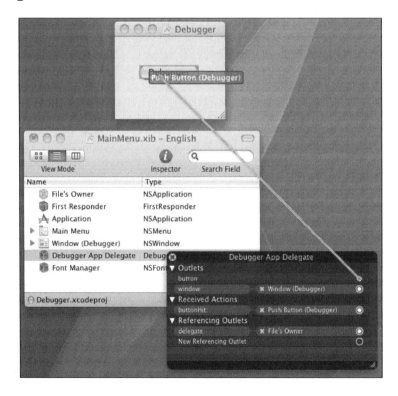

10. Back in Xcode, choose **Build and Run** from the toolbar to run the application.

How it works...

When you click the **Debugger** button in our sample application, the `buttonHit:` method is invoked and we begin iterating through the *for* loop statement. When the loop's *i* variable is equal to `200`, we call the `Debugger()` function which immediately causes the application to be interrupted in GDB. Note that you will see the message **Debugger() was called!** on the console of the debugger:

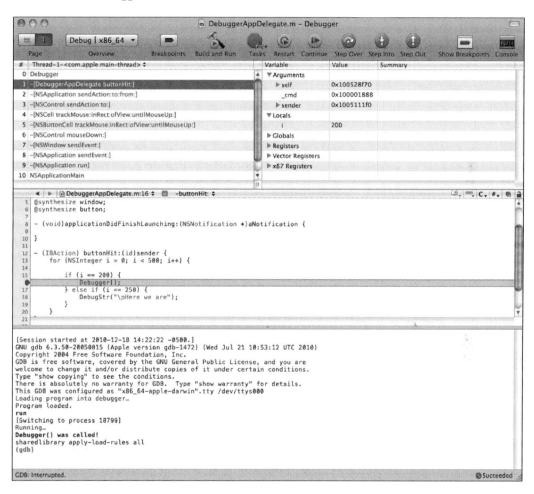

Typing *continue* or clicking on the **Continue** button in the toolbar will continue the loop until *i* is equal to 250 and the `DebugStr()` method is called, which will interrupt the application. Note that `DebugStr()` takes a pascal string as a parameter that will be printed in the debuggers console. To create a pascal string, you will need to prefix the string with \p as we have done in the example:

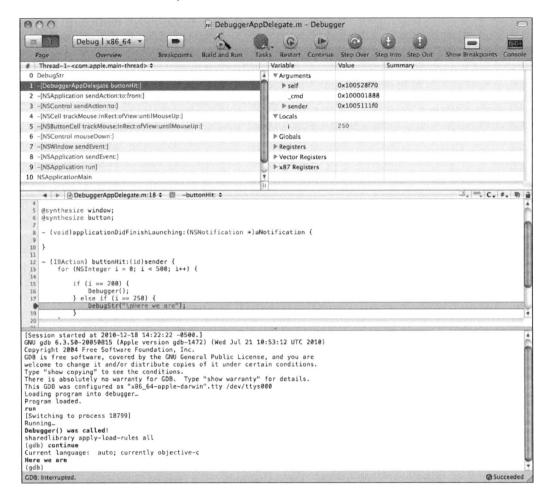

There's more...

When you use the `Debugger()` or `DebugStr()` functions to stop your application in the debugger, the stack will be pointing at whichever method was used to stop the debugger. In order to see your local variables in the debugger, you will need to click on the previous stack frame. In our example above, you would click on the –**[DebuggerAppDelegate buttonHit:]** stack frame.

In order for `Debugger()` and `DebugStr()` to break into the debugger, make sure that you have **Break on Debugger() and DebugStr()** selected on the **Debugging** tab of your applications Get Info dialog. The Get Info dialog for our sample application is shown below:

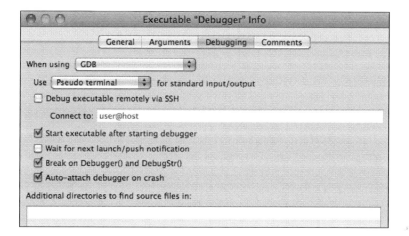

The sample code and project for this recipe is located under the `Debugger` folder in the code bundled with this book.

Using Build and Analyze in Xcode

Xcode now includes a tool to analyze your source code. In this recipe, we will use the Build and Analyze command to find an intentional memory leak to show you how the analyze command shows you exactly where the leak occurred.

Getting ready

In Xcode, create a new Cocoa Application project and name it **Analyze**.

How to do it...

1. Click on the `AnalyzeAppDelegate.h` to open it.

2. Add the method declaration for the `showErrorMessage:` method:

    ```
    - (void) showErrorMessage:(NSInteger)error;
    ```

3. Click on the `AnalyzeAppDelegate.m` to open it.

4. In the `applicationDidFinishLaunching:` method, add a call to the `showErrorMessage:` method:

   ```
   [self showErrorMessage:100];
   ```

5. Finally, add the `showErrorMessage:` method:

   ```
   - (void) showErrorMessage:(NSInteger)error {
     NSString *message = [[NSString alloc] init];

     if (error == 0) {
       message = [message stringByAppendingFormat:@"No error"];
     } else if (error == 100) {
       message = [message stringByAppendingFormat:@"Error code: %d",
         error];
     } else {
       message = [message stringByAppendingFormat:@"No error code
         specified"];
     }

     NSLog(@"%@", message);
   }
   ```

6. From the **Build** menu, choose **Build and Analyze**.

How it works...

The `showErrorMessage:` method creates an `NSString` to format the error code being passed into the method. We intentionally did not release the message variable to illustrate how Build and Analyze works. You can see from the screenshot below that the leaked string was found and that if we expand the analyze error, it will even show us the flow through the `showErrorMessage:` method:

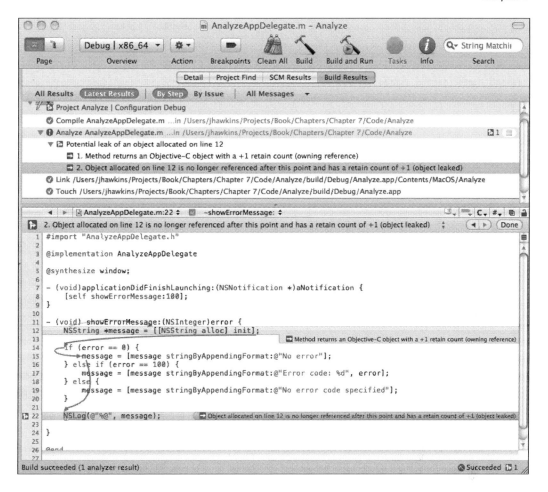

There's more...

When correcting the issues found by Build and Analyze, it is important to clean all targets before running Build and Analyze again. If you do not clean before re-running Build and Analyze, the source will not be analyzed and you might think that you have corrected all the issues.

See also

The sample code and project for this recipe is located under the `Analyze` folder in the code bundled with this book.

8
System Integration

In this chapter, we will cover:

- ▶ Adding a Badge to your Dock icon
- ▶ Adding a Menu to your Dock icon
- ▶ Creating a disk image for your application
- ▶ Updating your application with Sparkle

Introduction

In this chapter, we will discuss recipes that will integrate your application with OS X. We will also show how you can update your applications by integrating the Sparkle framework into your application.

 Some recipes in this chapter require Mac OS X Snow Leopard 10.6.

Adding a Badge to your Dock icon

In this recipe, we will add a badge to our application's dock icon. Adding or updating the badge is a way to provide feedback to the user if your application is running in the background.

Getting ready

In Xcode, create a new Cocoa Application project and name it Badge.

How to do it...

1. Click on `BadgeAppDelegate.m` to open it.

2. Add the following code to the `applicationDidFinishLaunching:` method:

   ```
   NSDockTile *dockTile = [NSApp dockTile];
   [dockTile setBadgeLabel:@"10"];
   [dockTile display];
   ```

3. Choose **Build and Run** from the toolbar to run the application:

How it works...

In order for a badge to display on the dock tile, we get the dock tile from the `NSApp` instance by calling the `dockTile:` method.

Next, we set the dock tile's badge label by calling `setBadgeLabel:` and call the display method to redraw the dock tile's content.

There's more...

You can also get a window's dock tile and provide a custom view and a badge label that will be displayed when a window is minimized.

See also

The sample code and project for this recipe is located under the `Badge` folder in the code bundled with this book.

Adding a Menu to your Dock icon

In this recipe, we will add a menu to our application's dock icon. By adding a menu to your application's dock icon, you can provide quick access to commonly used features.

Getting ready

In Xcode, create a new Cocoa Application project and name it `Menu`.

How to do it...

1. Click on `MenuAppDelegate.m` to open it.

2. Add the following method to the `MenuAppDelegate` class implementation:

```
- (NSMenu *)applicationDockMenu:(NSApplication *)sender {
    NSMenu *menu = [[[NSMenu alloc] initWithTitle:@"DocTile Menu"]
      autorelease];

    NSMenuItem *item = [[[NSMenuItem alloc] initWithTitle:@"Hello"
      action:@selector(hello) keyEquivalent:@"k"] autorelease];
    [menu addItem:item];

    return menu;
}
```

3. Next, add the hello method:

```
- (void) hello {
    [[NSAlert alertWithMessageText:@"Hello!" defaultButton:@"OK"
      alternateButton:nil otherButton:nil
      informativeTextWithFormat:@"Hello Message!"] runModal];
}
```

4. Choose **Build and Run** from the toolbar to run the application:

How it works...

The NSApplicationDelegate protocol defines the applicationDockMenu: method that we implement to create a dock menu dynamically within our application. Within the applicationDockMenu:, we create and return an autoreleased NSMenu with the NSMenuItems we need for our application. In our example, we created a single menu item that when chosen displays an alert.

There's more...

You can also create your dock menu within Interface Builder. Once you have created your menu, simply connect it to the **dockMenu** outlet on the **Application** object:

See also

The sample code and project for this recipe is located under the Menu folder in the code bundled with this book.

Creating a disk image for your application

In this recipe, we will create a disk image file for distributing your application. Although some developers distribute their applications as a compressed zip file, a disk image is a more professional way to package your application and support files.

Getting ready

Although there is not much needed to create a disk image, you will need a release build of your application and any supporting files such as a readme, and so on.

How to do it...

1. Start the `DiskUtility.app` located in the `Utilities` folder inside the `Applications` folder.

2. Choose **New Image** from the toolbar.

3. Enter a file name and choose a location for your disk image.

4. Next, enter a **Name** for the new image.

5. Set **Size** to **100 MB**. You can select a larger size if your application requires more than 100 MB

6. Set **Format** to **Mac OS Extended (Journaled)**.

7. Set **Encryption** to **none**.

8. Choose **Single partition – Apple Partition Map** for the **Partitions** popup.

9. Choose **read/write disk image** for the **Image Format** popup.

10. Click on **Create**:

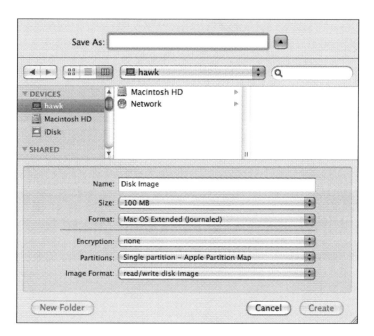

11. Return to the Finder and double-click on the disk image you just created to mount it.

12. You can now drag your application and any supporting files into the mounted disk image.

13. Most developers include an alias to the `Applications` folder in their disk image files so that the user can simply drag the application onto the alias to install the application in the users `Applications` folder.

14. Using the Finder's **Show View Options**, you can customize the background of the disk image with a custom color or image:

15. After you have modified the disk image, open the image in the `Disk Utility.app`

16. Select your disk image in the left pane and from the toolbar choose **Convert**.

17. Type a new name for your disk image and choose **Compressed** for the **Image Format**.

How it works...

The `DiskUtility.app` makes it quite easy to create disk images. It is important that the disk image is created with the correct **Mac OS Extended (Journaled) format**. In order to modify the disk image after it has been created, make sure that you have chosen **read/write disk image** in the **Image Format** popup.

There's more...

You might consider building the disk image from Xcode as part of your application's build process. You can use the *hdiutil* command line utility to create the disk images similar to those created with the `Disk Utility.app`.

See also

The *hdiutil* man page contains information regarding the options available to create disk images via the command line. For example, you can use the following command within `Terminal.app` to view the manual page for the *hdiutil* command:

```
hawk:~ jhawkins$ man hdiutil
```

Updating your application With Sparkle

In this recipe, we will show you how you can use the Sparkle framework to handle the updating of your application. Sparkle works by periodically checking your website for updates by reading a special `appcast.xml` file.

Getting ready

First, you will need to download the Sparkle framework from `http://sparkle.andymatuschak.org`.

Next, in Xcode, create a new Cocoa Application project and name it `Update`.

How to do it...

1. Expand the Frameworks group in the Xcode project view.

2. Right-click on **Linked Frameworks** and choose **Add...**, then choose **Existing Frameworks**. As an alternative, you can drag-and-drop the **Sparkle.framework** on the **Linked Frameworks** group to add it to the project.

3. Click on the **Add Other...** button and navigate to your downloaded Sparkle folder.

4. Select the **Sparkle.framework** and choose **Add**.

5. Expand the **Targets** group in the Xcode project view.

6. Right-click and choose **Add...**, then choose **New Build Phase** and finally choose **New Copy Files Build Phase**.

7. From the **Destination** popup, select **Frameworks**.

8. Drag the **Sparke.framework** from the **Linked Frameworks** group to the **Copy Files Build Phase** you just created.

9. Double click on `MainMenu.xib` to open it in Interface Builder.

10. From the Library palette in Interface Builder, drag an Object to your `MainMenu.xib` window. The Object can be found under the **Object & Controllers** section.

11. Choose the **Identity** tab from Interface Builder's **Inspector** palette and set the **Class** popup to **SUUpdater**.

12. Double-click on the **Main Menu** object in the `MainMenu.xib` window.

13. Click on the **Update** menu to expand it and drag a **MenuItem** from the **Library** palette to the **Update** menu just above the **Preferences...** menu item.

14. Rename the **MenuItem** to **Check for Updates...**

15. Right-click on the **Updater** object in the `MainMenu.xib` window and drag a connection from the `checkForUpdates:` action to the **Check for Updates...** menu item:

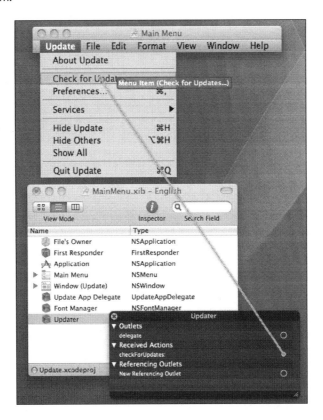

16. In Xcode, double-click the `Update-Info.plist` to open it and add a new row.

17. Set the key for the new row to **SUFeedURL** and set the value to the URL where your `appcast.xml` file will live on your web server.

18. Lastly, make sure your Bundle versions string is correct. It should only contain numbers and a period:

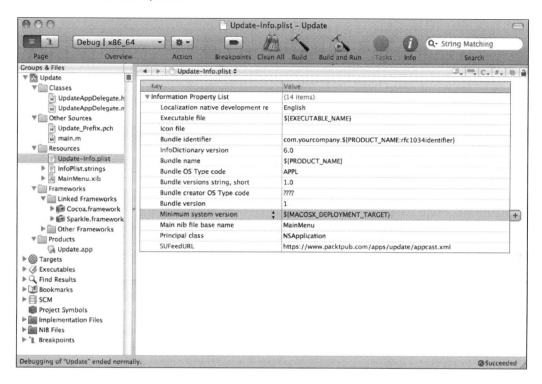

19. Choose **Build and Run** from the toolbar to run the application.

20. You will need to run your application a second time to test if the update is working correctly as Sparkle checks for updates on the second launch of the application.

How it works...

Now that you have incorporated Sparkle into your application, it will periodically check the `appcast.xml` file on your website to see if there is a new version.

When you are ready to create a new version of your application, you should update the bundle version so that it is greater than the current version. You should also compress the update and upload it to your web server.

Next, you need to edit the `appcast.xml` so that it reflects the new version of your application. It's best to start with the sample `appcast.xml` file located in the **Extras** folder of the Sparkle download and modify it for your application:

```
<item>
  <title>Version 1.2</title>
  <sparkle:releaseNotesLink>
    https://www.packtpub.com/apps/1.2.html
  </sparkle:releaseNotesLink>
  <pubDate>Wed, 06 Jan 2011 15:00:00 +0000</pubDate>
  <enclosure  url="https://www.packtpub.com/apps/update.1.2.zip"
    sparkle:version="1.2" length="433526" type="application/octet-
    stream" />
</item>
```

Basically, you need to add a new `item` element to the `appcast.xml` that describes your update. Once you have edited the `appcast.xml`, you need to upload it to your web server at the same path you set in the **SUFeedURL** bundle key in your `Update-Info.plist` file.

There's more...

To ensure a secure download and update, you have two options when using the Sparkle framework. You can use SSL and https to link to your web server or you can use the scripts included in the Sparkle `Extras` folder to sign your compressed application update. If you decide to sign your update, refer to the Sparkle documentation on how to generate the public and private keys and how to incorporate the public key into your updates bundle.

See also

To download the Sparkle framework or read the developer documentation, visit `http://sparkle.andymatuschak.org`.

9
Working with Files

In this chapter, we will cover:

- ▶ Saving your class with NSKeyedArchiver
- ▶ Loading your class with NSKeyedUnarchiver
- ▶ Finding special folders
- ▶ Basic XML parsing
- ▶ Parsing JSON

Introduction

This chapter will cover various ways in which you can work with files. We will create a Data class that be serialized to and from disk using the NSKeyedArchiver and NSKeyedUnarchiver classes. We will look at how we can locate special folders, such as the user's home directory, the Documents folder and the Library folder. Lastly, we will look at parsing both XML and JSON formatted files.

 Some recipes in this chapter require Mac OS X Snow Leopard 10.6.

Saving your class with NSKeyedArchiver

In this recipe, we will create a Data class that implements the NSCoding protocol to archive the Data class to disk using NSKeyedArchiver class.

Getting ready

In Xcode, create a new Cocoa Application project and name it `Saving`.

How to do it...

1. Right-click on the Xcode project view and choose **Add...**, then choose **New File**. Under the **Mac OS X** section, choose **Cocoa Class** and select **Objective-C class**. In the **Subclass of** popup, select `NSObject`. Click on **Next** and name the new class `Data.m`.

2. Click on `Data.h` to open it and add the following variables:

```
NSInteger version;
NSDate *date;
NSMutableArray *names;
```

3. Add properties for each of the above variables:

```
@property (assign) NSInteger version;
@property (retain) NSDate *date;
@property (retain) NSMutableArray *names;
```

4. Click on `Data.m` file to open it.

5. Synthesize the variables that we added to the class interface:

```
@synthesize version;
@synthesize date;
@synthesize names;
```

6. Add the following `encodeWithCoder:` method for encoding the variables in our Data class:

```
- (void) encodeWithCoder:(NSCoder *)encoder {
    [encoder encodeInteger:[self version] forKey:@"version"];
    [encoder encodeObject:date forKey:@"date"];
    [encoder encodeObject:names forKey:@"names"];
}
```

7. Next, add the `initWithCoder:` method for instantiating our class from an archive:

```
- (id) initWithCoder:(NSCoder *)decoder {
    self = [super init];
    if (self != nil) {
        version = [decoder decodeIntegerForKey:@"version"];
        date = [[decoder decodeObjectForKey:@"date"] retain];
        names = [[[NSMutableArray alloc] initWithArray:[decoder
            decodeObjectForKey:@"names"]] retain];
    }

    return self;
}
```

8. Click on the `SavingAppDelegate.m` class to open it.

9. Add an import for our Data class:

    ```
    #import "Data.h"
    ```

10. Add the following code to the `applicationDidFinishLaunching:` method:

    ```
    Data *data = [[Data alloc] init];
    [data setVersion:1];
    [data setDate:[NSDate new]];

    NSMutableArray *array = [[NSMutableArray alloc] init];
    [array addObject:@"Ben Franklin"];
    [array addObject:@"Sam Adams"];
    [array addObject:@"George Washington"];

    [data setNames:array];

    NSArray *applicationSupportPaths =
    NSSearchPathForDirectoriesInDomains(NSApplicationSupportDirectory,
      NSUserDomainMask, YES);
      NSString *path = [applicationSupportPaths objectAtIndex:0];
    path = [path stringByAppendingPathComponent:@"Packt Publishing"];
    [[NSFileManager defaultManager] createDirectoryAtPath:path
      withIntermediateDirectories:YES attributes:nil error:NULL];
    path = [path
      stringByAppendingPathComponent:@"SavedDataObject.data"];
      [NSKeyedArchiver archiveRootObject:data toFile:path];
    ```

11. Choose **Build and Run** from the toolbar to run the application.

How it works...

To archive a class, you need to add the `NSCoding` protocol in your classes interface and then implement the `encodeWithCoder:` method, which will be called by the `NSKeyedArchiver` class when archiving your object. The `NSCoder` class provides several methods to encode all standard types and most, if not all Cocoa objects. To encode a field, you need to select the proper encode method, such as `encodeInteger:`, `encodeFloat:`, or `encodeObject:` for the field type that you are encoding and provide a key which will be used to decode the field when the `initWithCoder:` method is called when unarchiving the archive.

There's more...

It is usually a good idea to encode a version number into the object you are archiving to support future enhancements and backward compatibility. This can be done by simply encoding an `NSInteger` as shown in the example above. You can then check the version number when decoding to decide which objects need to be unarchived.

Also note that `NSCoder` cannot encode unions, void pointers, or function pointers.

See also

The sample code and project for this recipe is located under the `Saving` folder in the code bundled with this book.

Loading your class with NSKeyedUnarchiver

In this recipe, we will load the archived `Data` class that we saved to disk in the *Saving your class with NSKeyedArchiver* recipe.

Getting ready

This recipe uses the data file `SavedDataObject.data`, created from the *Saving your class with NSKeyedArchiver* recipe. In order for this recipe's sample application to work correctly, you will need to run the sample application from the *Saving your class with NSKeyedArchiver* first to generate the data file in your home directory.

To begin, start Xcode and create a new Cocoa Application project and name it `Loading`.

How to do it...

1. Right-click on the Xcode project view and choose **Add...**, then choose **New File**. Under the **Mac OS X** section, choose **Cocoa Class** and select **Objective-C class**. In the **Subclass of** popup, select `NSObject`. Click on **Next** and name the new class `Data.m`.

   Note that we are using the same `Data` class that we created in the *Saving your Class with NSCoder* recipe above.

2. Click on `Data.h` to open it and add the following variables:
   ```
   NSInteger version;
   NSDate *date;
   NSMutableArray *names;
   ```

3. Add properties for each of the above variables:

```
@property (assign) NSInteger version;
@property (retain) NSDate *date;
@property (retain) NSMutableArray *names;
```

4. Click on `Data.m` file to open it.

5. Synthesize the variables that we added to the class interface:

```
@synthesize version;
@synthesize date;
@synthesize names;
```

6. Add the following `encodeWithCoder:` method for encoding the variables in our Data class:

```
- (void) encodeWithCoder:(NSCoder *)encoder {
    [encoder encodeInteger:[self version] forKey:@"version"];
    [encoder encodeObject:date forKey:@"date"];
    [encoder encodeObject:names forKey:@"names"];
}
```

7. Next, add the `initWithCoder:` method for instantiating our class from an archive:

```
- (id) initWithCoder:(NSCoder *)decoder {
    self = [super init];
    if (self != nil) {
        version = [decoder decodeIntegerForKey:@"version"];
        date = [[decoder decodeObjectForKey:@"date"] retain];
        names = [[[NSMutableArray alloc] initWithArray:[decoder
            decodeObjectForKey:@"names"]] retain];
    }

    return self;
}
```

8. Click on the `LoadingAppDelegate.m` class to open it.

9. Add an import for our Data class:

```
#import "Data.h"
```

10. Add the following code to the `applicationDidFinishLaunching:` method:

```
NSArray *applicationSupportPaths =
NSSearchPathForDirectoriesInDomains(NSApplicationSupportDirectory,
    NSUserDomainMask, YES);
NSString *path = [applicationSupportPaths objectAtIndex:0];
path = [path stringByAppendingPathComponent:@"Packt Publishing"];
[[NSFileManager defaultManager] createDirectoryAtPath:path
    withIntermediateDirectories:YES attributes:nil error:NULL];
```

```
path = [path
  stringByAppendingPathComponent:@"SavedDataObject.data"];
Data *data = [NSKeyedUnarchiver unarchiveObjectWithFile:path];

NSLog(@"Version: %d", [data version]);
NSLog(@"   Date: %@", [data date]);

NSArray *array = [data names];
for (NSString *name in array) {
  NSLog(@"   Name: %@", name);
}
```

11. Choose **Build and Run** from the toolbar to run the application.

12. View the console to see the output from running the application. You will notice that the values are the same as the values saved in the *Saving your Class with NSKeyedArchiver* recipe above.

How it works...

To load the `Data` class archive from disk, the `NSKeyedUnarchiver` class will call the `Data` class' `initWithCoder:` method at which point we can use the `NSCoder` passed into the method to decode the classes fields using the same key names we used in the `encodeWithCoder:` method.

There's more...

When decoding object types, it is important to remember to retain the returned object from the `decodeObjectForKey:` method as you will be receiving an autoreleased object.

See also

The sample code and project for this recipe is located under the `Loading` folder in the code bundled with this book.

Finding special folders

Mac OS X has many special folders, which are used for organizing data. The Cocoa foundation provides the `NSSearchPathForDirectoriesInDomains()` method and many pre-defined enumerations to locate these directories. In this recipe, we will locate some of the more common folders using the methods provided by Cocoa.

Getting ready

In Xcode, create a new Cocoa Application project and name it `SpecialFolders`.

How to do it...

1. Click on SpecialFoldersAppDelegate.m to open it.

2. Add the following code to the `applicationDidFinishingLaunching:` method:

```
NSArray *paths =
  NSSearchPathForDirectoriesInDomains(NSLibraryDirectory,
  NSUserDomainMask, YES);
if ([paths count] > 0) {
  NSLog(@"User Library Directory: %@", [paths objectAtIndex:0]);
}

paths = NSSearchPathForDirectoriesInDomains(NSDocumentDirectory,
  NSUserDomainMask, YES);
if ([paths count] > 0) {
  NSLog(@"User Documents Directory: %@", [paths objectAtIndex:0]);
}

paths = NSSearchPathForDirectoriesInDomains(NSDownloadsDirectory,
  NSUserDomainMask, YES);
if ([paths count] > 0) {
  NSLog(@"User Downloads Directory: %@", [paths objectAtIndex:0]);
}

paths = NSSearchPathForDirectoriesInDomains(NSAllApplicationsDirec
tory,
  NSAllDomainsMask, YES);
for (NSString *path in paths) {
  NSLog(@"%@", path);
}

NSString *homeDirectory = NSHomeDirectory();
NSLog(@"Users Home Directory: %@", homeDirectory);

homeDirectory = NSHomeDirectoryForUser(@"shawkins");
NSLog(@"Users Home Directory: %@", homeDirectory);
```

3. Choose **Build and Run** from the toolbar to run the application.

4. View the console to see the output from the application.

How it works...

To locate folders in Cocoa, we use the NSSearchPathForDirectoriesInDomains() method which returns an NSArray of paths. In some cases, based on the passed domain mask, this method will return only a single path, but for others it is possible to have many paths returned. In the above example, we are interested in finding the current user's Documents directory, so we use the NSUserDomainMask as the domain and the NSDocumentDirectory as the search path directory. In this case, the returned array will contain a single path to the current user's Documents directory.

If we needed to find all the directories where applications are stored, we could pass NSAllApplicationsDirectory as the search path directory and NSAllDomainsMask as the domain mask. The resulting array would contain paths similar to the following:

```
/Users/jhawkins/Applications
/Users/jhawkins/Applications/Utilities
/Users/jhawkins/Developer/Applications
/Users/jhawkins/Applications/Demos
/Applications
/Applications/Utilities
/Developer/Applications
/Applications/Demos
/Network/Applications
/Network/Applications/Utilities
/Network/Developer/Applications
/Network/Applications/Demos
```

There are two other useful methods provided by Cocoa for locating a user's home directory. NSHomeDirectory() is used for finding the path to the current user's home directory. The other method, NSHomeDirectoryForUser() can be used to locate the path for a user's home directory if you know the users login name.

There's more...

Note that the paths returned from NSSearchPathForDirectoriesInDomains() may not actually exist on disk and therefore you will need to use the NSFileManager to check the existence of a directory before writing to it or reading from it.

See also

The sample code and project for this recipe is located under the SpecialFolders folder in the code bundled with this book.

Basic XML parsing

With more and more applications interacting with third party services via API's, and the transfer of data in the XML format, it is common to have a need to parse XML. In this recipe, we will show the basics of parsing a simple XML file for element data and attribute data.

Getting ready

In Xcode, create a new Cocoa Application project and name it XML.

How to do it...

1. Right-click on the Xcode project and choose **Add...**, then choose **New File....** In the **New File** dialog, choose **Other** from the **Mac OS X** section and choose **Empty File** and click **Next**. Name the file models.xml.

2. Click on the models.xml file to open it and add the following XML:

```
<?xml version="1.0" encoding="utf-8"?>
<models>
  <model type="laptop">
    MacBook Pro
  </model>
  <model type="laptop">
    MacBook
  </model>
  <model type="desktop">
    iMac
  </model>
  <model type="desktop">
    Mac Mini
  </model>
</models>
```

3. Click on XMLAppDelegate.m to open it.

4. Add the following code to the applicationDidFinishLaunching: method:

```
NSString *path = [[NSBundle mainBundle] pathForResource:@"models"
  ofType:@"xml"];
path = [path stringByAddingPercentEscapesUsingEncoding:
NSUTF8StringEncoding];

NSURL *url = [NSURL URLWithString:[NSString
  stringWithFormat:@"file://%@", path]];
```

```
NSError *error;
NSXMLDocument *document = [[NSXMLDocument alloc]
    initWithContentsOfURL:url options:NSXMLDocumentTidyXML
    error:&error];

NSXMLElement *rootElement = [document rootElement];
if (rootElement != nil) {
  NSArray *models = [rootElement elementsForName:@"model"];
  if (models != nil) {
    for (NSXMLElement *element in models) {
      NSXMLNode *type = [element attributeForName:@"type"];
      NSLog(@"Model: %@ Type: %@", [element stringValue], [type
        stringValue]);
    }
  }
}

[document release];
```

5. Choose **Build and Run** from the toolbar to run the application.

6. View the console to see the output from the application.

How it works...

In the example above, we are loading the XML document located in the bundle of the application. Since this path may have spaces within it, we must escape the path as it will be used in a URL. We call the `stringByAddingPercentEscapesUsingEncoding:` method in the `NSString` class to handle the escaping of the path. Next, we create a `NSURL` that we can pass to the `initWithContentsOfURL:` method of `NSXMLDocument`.

Once we have a reference to the document, we can get an `NSArray` of model elements by using the `elementsForName:` method. As we loop over the returned elements, we can get the text of the element using the `stringValue` method of `NSXMLElement` class.

In our example, we need to retrieve the type of model from the type attribute on the model element. To do this, we call the `attributeForName:` method on the model element passing the name of the attribute that we are interested in. In this case, it is *type*. The `attributeForName:` method returns an `NSXMLNode`, so to get the value of the attribute we need to call the `stringValue` method.

There's more...

You may be wondering why some methods return `NSXMLElement`'s and other methods return `NSXMLNode`'s. An `NSXMLElement` represents an actual element with the XML structure, whereas `NSXMLNode`'s are the base class for all types of items within XML such as attributes, text, and even elements.

See also

The sample code and project for this recipe is located under the `XML` folder in the code bundled with this book.

Parsing JSON

More and more applications are using JSON to transfer data over the Internet due to its simplicity and lighter weight. In this recipe, we will use an open source parser named TouchJSON to parse a simple JSON formatted file.

Note that we have used the same data in our JSON file as we did in the previous recipe, *Basic XML Parsing*, so you can see the differences in complexity.

Getting ready

In Xcode, create a new Cocoa Application project and name it `JSON`.

How to do it...

1. Download the TouchJSON open source JSON parser project from
   `https://github.com/TouchCode/TouchJSON`.

2. Locate the downloaded TouchJSON project and drag the Source folder into your Xcode project.

3. Right-click on the Xcode project and choose **Add...**, then choose **New File...**. In the **New File** dialog, choose **Other** from the **Mac OS X** section and choose **Empty File** and click **Next**. Name the file `models.json`.

4. Click on the `models.json` file to open it and add the following json:

```
{
    "models" : [
        {
            "model" : "MacBook Pro",
            "type" : "laptop"
        },
```

```
      {
          "model" : "MacBook",
          "type" : "laptop"
      },
      {
          "model" : "iMac",
          "type" : "desktop"
      },
      {
          "model" : "Mac Mini",
          "type" : "desktop"
      }
    ],
}
```

5. Click on `JSONAppDelegate.m` to open it.

6. Add an import for the JSON deserializer. This header file is located in the TouchJSON Source folder:

   ```
   #import "CJSONDeserializer.h"
   ```

7. Add the following code to the `applicationDidFinishLaunching:` method:

   ```
   NSString *path = [[NSBundle mainBundle] pathForResource:@"models"
       ofType:@"json"];
   NSData *json = [NSData dataWithContentsOfFile:path];

   NSError *error = nil;
   NSDictionary *dictionary = [[CJSONDeserializer deserializer]
       deserializeAsDictionary:json error:&error];

   NSArray *models = [dictionary objectForKey:@"models"];

   for (NSDictionary *model in models) {
       NSString *modelString = [model objectForKey:@"model"];
       NSString *typeString = [model objectForKey:@"type"];

       NSLog(@"Model: %@", modelString);
       NSLog(@"Type: %@", typeString);
   }
   ```

8. Choose **Build and Run** from the toolbar to run the application.

9. View the console to see the output from the application.

How it works...

Using the CJSONDeserializer class from TouchJSON, we call the
deserializeAsDictionary: method. Basically we are converting the JSON into an
NSDictionary. Next, using the *models* key, we get an array of models, each of type
NSDictionary. We loop over each of the models, getting the model and the type of Mac.

There's more...

As you can see from this example, using the TouchJSON classes to parse the JSON, we
work with familiar NSArray and NSDictionary classes, which simplify the use of JSON
even more.

See also

The sample code and project for this recipe is located under the JSON folder in the code
bundled with this book.

10

Working with the Web

In this chapter, we will cover:

- ▶ Using NSURLConnection with HTTP GET
- ▶ Using NSURLConnection with HTTP POST
- ▶ Adding a hex encoding category to NSData
- ▶ Adding a hex decoding category to NSString
- ▶ Adding a Base64 encoding category to NSData
- ▶ Adding a Base64 decoding category to NSString
- ▶ Adding a MD5 hash category to NSData
- ▶ Escaping a URL

Introduction

In this chapter, we will learn how to use Cocoa's classes to communicate over the web. We will take a look at using `NSURLConnection` to handle the GET and POST methods of HTTP. We will also extend the `NSData` and `NSString` classes with categories to handle some basic encoding and hashing. Finally, we will take a look at how to properly escape URLs using a specific Core Foundation method.

Using NSURLConnection with HTTP GET

In this recipe, we will use the NSURLConnection class to asynchronously retrieve the source of a web page.

Getting ready

In Xcode, create a new Cocoa Application project and name it HttpGet.

How to do it...

1. Click on HttpGetAppDelegate.h to open it.

2. Add the data variable to the class interface:

   ```
   NSMutableData *data;
   ```

3. Add the property definition for the data variable:

   ```
   @property (retain, nonatomic) NSMutableData *data;
   ```

4. Click on the HttpGetAppDelegate.m to open it.

5. Add the following code to the applicationDidFinishLaunching: method:

   ```
   NSString *address = [NSString
     stringWithFormat:@"http://www.google.com"];
   NSURL *url = [NSURL URLWithString:address];

   NSMutableURLRequest *request = [NSMutableURLRequest
     requestWithURL:url];
   [request setHTTPMethod:@"GET"];

   NSURLConnection *connection = [[NSURLConnection alloc]
     initWithRequest:request delegate:self];

   if (data == nil) {
     data = [[NSMutableData alloc] init];
   }

   [connection release];
   ```

6. Next, add the following delegate methods:

```
- (void) connection:(NSURLConnection *)connection
  didReceiveResponse:(NSURLResponse *)response
{
  [data setLength: 0];
}


- (void) connection:(NSURLConnection *)connection
  didReceiveData:(NSData *)inData
{
  [data appendData:inData];
}


- (void) connection:(NSURLConnection *)connection
  didFailWithError:(NSError *)error
{
  [data release];
}


- (void) connectionDidFinishLoading:(NSURLConnection *)connection
{
  if (data != nil && [data length] > 0) {
    NSString *value = [[[NSString alloc] initWithBytes:[data
      bytes] length:[data length] encoding:NSUTF8StringEncoding]
      autorelease];
    NSLog(@"%@", value);
  }

  [data release];
}
```

7. Choose **Build and Run** from the toolbar to run the application.

8. View the console to see the output from running the application.

How it works...

In this recipe, we are making a request to `www.google.com` asynchronously. We begin by creating an `NSMutableURLRequest` so that we can set the HTTP method to be used. In this case, we are using the GET method. In the class interface, we have defined a data variable as an `NSMutableData`, which we will append to as the data is received from the request.

We set the `HttpGetAppDelegate` class as the delegate for `NSURLConnection`. As `NSURLConnection` progresses through the various stages of making the request and returning the response, our delegate methods will be called to notify us of progress, errors, and data received.

When the request is complete, the `connectionDidFinishLoading:` delegate method will be called, which will signal the end of the request. In this recipe, we simply print the data that we received to the console.

There's more...

Using the `NSURLConnection` class, you can also perform synchronous requests by using the `sendSynchronousRequest:` method. The next recipe, *Using NSURLConnection With HTTP POST* demonstrates how to use this method to post data.

See also

The sample code and project for this recipe is located under the `HttpGet` folder in the code bundled with this book.

Using NSURLConnection with HTTP POST

`NSURLConnection` can also be used synchronously to handle requests. In this recipe, we will send data using `NSURLConnection` and the HTTP POST method.

 This recipe requires you to turn on Web Sharing so that we can POST data to a PHP script running on the local Apache server included with Mac OS X. You may need to enable PHP on your computer before you are able to run this recipe. The following link contains step-by-step details on configuring Apache to run PHP scripts: `http://foundationphp.com/tutorials/php_leopard.php`.

Getting ready

In Xcode, create a new Cocoa Application project and name it `HttpPost`.

How to do it...

1. Click on `HttpPostAppDelegate.m` to open it.

2. Add the following code to the `applicationDidFinishLaunching:` method:

```
NSURL *url = [NSURL
  URLWithString:@"http://localhost/~jhawkins/post.php"];
NSMutableURLRequest *request = [[[NSMutableURLRequest alloc]
  initWithURL:url] autorelease];
[request addValue:@"application/x-www-form-urlencoded"
  forHTTPHeaderField:@"Content-Type"];
[request setHTTPMethod:@"POST"];

NSString *body = @"This is some sample post data.";
NSData *postData = [[[NSData alloc] initWithBytes:[body
  UTF8String] length:[body length]] autorelease];
[request setHTTPBody:postData];

NSHTTPURLResponse *response = nil;
NSError *error = nil;

[NSURLConnection sendSynchronousRequest:request
  returningResponse:&response error:&error];

NSLog(@"Status Code: %d", [response statusCode]);
```

3. Next, create a `post.php` file in the `Sites` directory of your home directory.

4. Add the following code to the `post.php` file:

```php
<?php
  $data = file_get_contents("php://input");
  error_log($data, 3, "/tmp/errors.log");

  header("Status: 200 OK");
?>
```

5. Make sure that you have enabled **Web Sharing** in the **System Preferences**:

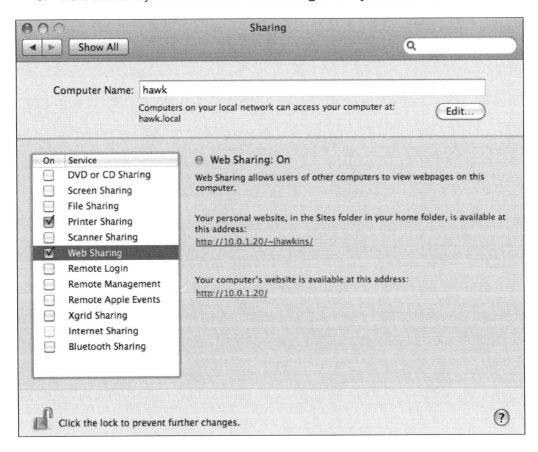

6. Choose **Build and Run** from the toolbar to run the application.

7. Using the `Terminal.app`, `cd` to `/tmp` and view the `errors.log` file.
   The `errors.log` file will contain the output from the PHP script.

How it works...

First, we create an `NSMutableURLRequest` with a URL pointing to the PHP script running on our local host. Note that the URL includes the name of my home directory. You will need to modify this to use the name of your home directory. Next, we set the content type header so that the PHP script is aware of the type of data we are sending it. We set the HTTP method to *POST* and set the HTTP body to the data that we would like to post to the PHP script. In this recipe, we are sending a short string of text.

Finally, we call the `sendSynchronousRequest:` method, passing in our request. When this method returns, we can check the status code returned in the `NSHTTPURLResponse` to determine if the posting of the data was successful.

To verify that the data was posted to the PHP script, you can open the `errors.log` file in the `/tmp` directory.

There's more...

If you need to authenticate a user, either while posting or getting data, you will need to call `NSURLConnection` asynchronously to properly handle the authentication challenge by using the `didReceiveAuthenticationChallenge:` delegate method.

See also

The sample code and project for this recipe is located under the `HttpPost` folder in the code bundled with this book.

Adding a hex encoding category to NSData

In this recipe, we will add a hex encoding method to the `NSData` class by creating a category on the `NSData` class.

Getting ready

In Xcode, create a new Cocoa Application project and name it `HexEncode`.

How to do it...

1. Click on `HexEncodeAppDelegate.h` to open it.
2. Add the following interface to create a category on the `NSData` class:

    ```
    @interface NSData (HEX)
    - (NSString *) bytesToHex;
    @end
    ```

3. Click on the `HexEncodeAppDelegate.m` to open it.
4. Add the code given below to create the `bytesToHex:` method for our category on the NSData class:

    ```
    @implementation NSData (HEX)

    - (NSString *) bytesToHex {
      NSMutableString *buffer = [NSMutableString
    ```

```
            stringWithCapacity:([self length] * 2)];
        const unsigned char *bytes = [self bytes];

        for (NSInteger i = 0; i < [self length]; ++i) {
            [buffer appendFormat:@"%02x", (unsigned long)bytes[i]];
        }

        return buffer;
    }

    @end
```

5. Next, add the following to the `applicationDidFinishLaunching:` method:

```
NSString *name = @"Packt Publishing";
NSData *data = [[[NSData alloc] initWithBytes:[name UTF8String]
    length:[name length]] autorelease];

NSString *hex = [data bytesToHex];
NSLog(@"Hex String: %@", hex);
```

6. Choose **Build and Run** from the toolbar to run the application.

7. View the console to see the output from running the application.

How it works...

Since the data that we need to convert to hex is held within the NSData object, we can create a convenience method on the NSData class to convert its bytes to hex. We handle this by creating a category on the NSData class that will hold our bytesToHex: method. This method simply takes the bytes and formats them using the NSMutablesString method appendFormat: using the hex format specifier.

See also

The sample code and project for this recipe is located under the HexEncode folder in the code bundled with this book.

Adding a hex decoding category to NSString

In this recipe, we will add a hex decoding method to the NSString class by creating a category on the NSString class.

Getting ready

In Xcode, create a new Cocoa Application project and name it HexDecode.

How to do it...

1. Click on HexDecodeAppDelegate.h to open it.

2. Add the following interface to add our category to the NSString class:

    ```
    @interface NSString (HEX)

    - (NSData *) hexToBytes;

    @end
    ```

3. Click on HexDecodeAppDelegate.m to open it.

4. Add the following implementation to add the hexToBytes: method to our NSString category:

    ```
    @implementation NSString (HEX)

    - (NSData *) hexToBytes {
      NSMutableData *data = [NSMutableData data];

      for (NSInteger index = 0; index + 2 <= [self length]; index +=
        2)
    {
        NSRange range = NSMakeRange(index, 2);
        NSString *hex = [self substringWithRange:range];
        NSScanner *scanner = [NSScanner scannerWithString:hex];
        unsigned intValue;
        [scanner scanHexInt:&intValue];

        [data appendBytes:&intValue length:1];
      }

      return data;
    }

    @end
    ```

5. Finally, add the following code to the `applicationDidFinishLaunching:` method:

```
NSString *hex = @"5061636b74205075626c697368696e67";
NSData *data = [hex hexToBytes];
NSString *value = [[[NSString alloc] initWithBytes:[data bytes]
    length:[data length] encoding:NSUTF8StringEncoding]
    autorelease];
NSLog(@"Value: %@", value);
```

6. Choose **Build and Run** from the toolbar to run the application.

7. View the console to see the output from running the application.

How it works...

We begin by adding a category called HEX to the `NSString` class. This category will allow us to extend the `NSString` class and add our `hexToBytes:` method.

Within the `hexToBytes:` method, we create an `NSMutableData` variable to hold the decoded bytes. As we loop over the hex string, we take advantage of the `NSScanner` class provided by Cocoa to scan each hex as an integer. Finally, we append the integer as a byte of one to our mutable data.

See also

The sample code and project for this recipe is located under the `HexDecode` folder in the code bundled with this book.

Adding a Base64 encoding category to NSData

When exchanging data with other services, it is often necessary to encode binary data using Base64 encoding. This translates the binary data into an ASCII representation that can be safely transferred over the Internet. In this recipe, we will add a category to the `NSData` class, which will provide a method to encode `NSData` objects to Base64.

Getting ready

In Xcode, create a new Cocoa Application project and name it `Base64Encode`.

How to do it...

1. Click on `Base64EncodeAppDelegate.h` to open it.

2. Add an import for the openssl header file:

   ```
   #import <openssl/ssl.h>
   ```

3. Next, expand the **Frameworks** group.

4. Right-click on the **Linked Frameworks** and choose **Add...**, then choose **Existing Frameworks...**

5. Choose **Dylibs** from the popup at the top of the Frameworks dialog.

6. Select **libcrypto.dylib** and click on **Add**:

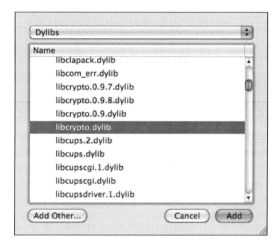

7. Add the following interface, which will add a category on the `NSData` class:

   ```
   @interface NSData (BASE64)
   - (NSString *) base64Encode;
   @end
   ```

8. Click on `Base64EncodeAppDelegate.m` to open it.

9. Add the following implementation of the `base64Encode:` method to the `NSData` category:

   ```
   @implementation NSData (BASE64)

   - (NSString *) base64Encode {
     BIO *buffer = BIO_new(BIO_s_mem());
     BIO *base64 = BIO_new(BIO_f_base64());

     buffer = BIO_push(base64, buffer);
   ```

```
        BIO_write(buffer, [self bytes], [self length]);
         BIO_flush(buffer);

        void *bytes;
          NSUInteger length = BIO_get_mem_data(buffer, &bytes);
        NSString *string =[[[NSString alloc] initWithBytes:bytes
           length:length encoding:NSUTF8StringEncoding] autorelease];

        BIO_free_all(buffer);

         return string;
    }

    @end
```

10. Add the code below to the `applicationDidFinishLaunching:` method:

```
    NSString *name = @"Packt Publishing";
    NSData *data = [NSData dataWithBytes:[name UTF8String]
      length:[name length]];
    NSString *base64 = [data base64Encode];
    NSLog(@"Base 64: %@", base64);
```

11. Choose **Build and Run** from the toolbar to run the application.

12. View the console to see the output from running the application.

How it works...

To encode the bytes to the Base64 ASCII representation, we add a category called BASE64 to the NSData class. The BASE64 category will add the base64Encode: method to the NSData class, which will use the OpenSSL library functions to handle the encoding.

The encoding begins by allocating a buffer and a base64 filter, which is pushed into the buffer. Now that the buffer is properly set up, any bytes that we write to the buffer will be converted to Base64. Once we finish writing the bytes and flush the buffer, we can get the length of the buffer, which we will use to create a new autoreleased NSString to return to the caller.

See also

The sample code and project for this recipe is located under the Base64Encode folder in the code bundled with this book.

Adding a Base64 decoding category to NSString

Base64 is a common encoding used by many third party services to convert binary data to ASCII for safe transport over the Internet. In this recipe we will add a method to decode Base64 to Cocoa's NSString class using a category.

Getting ready

In Xcode, create a new Cocoa Application project and name it Base64Decode.

How to do it...

1. Click on Base64DecodeAppDelegate.h to open it.

2. Add the interface for NSString:

    ```
    @interface NSString (BASE64)
    - (NSData *) base64Decode;
    @end
    ```

3. Click on Base64AppDelegate.m to open the implementation.

4. Add the import for openssl:

    ```
    #import <openssl/ssl.h>
    ```

5. Expand the **Frameworks** group.

6. Right-click on **Linked Frameworks** and choose **Add...**, then choose **Existing Frameworks**. Select **Dylibs** from the popup.

7. Select **libcrypto.dylib** and choose **Add**.

8. Add the following code for the implementation of the category on the NSString class:

    ```
    @implementation NSString (BASE64)

    - (NSData *) base64Decode {

      BIO *buffer = BIO_new_mem_buf((void *)[self UTF8String], [self
        length]);

      BIO *base64 = BIO_new(BIO_f_base64());
      buffer = BIO_push(base64, buffer);
      BIO_set_flags(base64, BIO_FLAGS_BASE64_NO_NL);
    ```

```
        NSMutableData *data = [NSMutableData data];
        char chars[512];

        int length = BIO_read(buffer, chars, sizeof(chars));
        while (length > 0) {
          [data appendBytes:chars length:length];

          length = BIO_read(buffer, chars, sizeof(chars));
        }

        BIO_free_all(buffer);

        return data;
    }

@end
```

9. Finally, add the code below to the `applicationDidFinishLaunching:` method:

```
NSString *base64 = @"UGFja3QgUHVibGlzaGluZw==";
NSData *data = [base64 base64Decode];

NSString *string = [[[NSString alloc] initWithData:data encoding:
NSUTF8StringEncoding] autorelease];
NSLog(@"name: %@", string);
```

10. Choose **Build and Run** from the toolbar to run the application.

11. View the console to see the output from running the application.

How it works...

We begin by creating a category on `NSString` called HEX. This category will hold our method to decode the base64 data. The method that we will be adding to `NSString` will be called base64Decode and is implemented using the `OpenSSL` libraries.

Basically, our decode method allocates a buffer containing the data from the `NSString`. We then allocate a base64 filter using the `BIO_new()` method and push that filter into the BIO buffer. Now, when we read from the BIO buffer, the data will be decoded for us and we can append it to our `NSMutableData` variable.

See also

The sample code and project for this recipe is located under the `Base64Decode` folder in the code bundled with this book.

Adding a MD5 hash category to NSData

Message-Digest algorithm 5 or MD5 is used to create a hash of a value. In this recipe, we will use the `OpenSSL` library to create a MD5 hash.

Getting ready

In Xcode, create a new Cocoa Application project and name it `MD5`.

How to do it...

1. Click on `MD5AppDelegate.h` to open it.
2. Add the interface below for the category on the `NSData` class:

   ```
   @interface NSData (MD5)
   - (NSData *) md5;
   @end
   ```

3. Click on `MD5AppDelegate.m` to open it.
4. Add the import for the openssl header file:

   ```
   #import <openssl/ssl.h>
   ```

5. Expand the **Frameworks** group.
6. Right-click on **Linked Frameworks** and choose **Add...**, then choose **Existing Frameworks**. Select **Dylibs** from the popup.
7. Select **libcrypto.dylib** and choose **Add**.
8. Add the implementation for the `md5:` method on the `NSData` category:

   ```
   @implementation NSData (MD5)

   - (NSData *) md5 {
     EVP_MD_CTX evp_md_ctx;
     unsigned char value[EVP_MAX_MD_SIZE];
     unsigned int length;

     EVP_DigestInit(&evp_md_ctx, EVP_md5());
     EVP_DigestUpdate(&evp_md_ctx, [self bytes], [self length]);
     EVP_DigestFinal(&evp_md_ctx, value, &length);

     return [NSData dataWithBytes:value length:length];
   }

   @end
   ```

9. Lastly, add the following code to the `applicationDidFinishLaunching:` method:

```
NSString *name = @"Packt Publishing";
NSData *data = [NSData dataWithBytes:[name UTF8String]
    length:[name length]];
data = [data md5];

NSString *md5 = @"";
unsigned char *bytes = (unsigned char *)[data bytes];
for (NSInteger i = 0; i < [data length]; i++) {
    md5 = [md5 stringByAppendingFormat:@"%02X", bytes[i]];
}

NSLog(@"MD5: %@", md5);
```

10. Choose **Build and Run** from the toolbar to run the application.

11. View the console to see the output from running the application.

How it works...

To handle the MD5 encoding, we create a category on the NSData class. To implement the md5: method, we use the library methods from the OpenSSL crypto.dylib.

Once we create the EVP_MD_CTX context and buffer, we initialize the context with the md5 hashing algorithm. We then call the EVP_DigestUpdate() function to update the context with the internal bytes from the NSData object. Lastly, we call the EVP_DigestFinal() function, which updates the buffer and the length variables with the details of the hash. Finally, we create a new autoreleased NSData object to return to the caller.

There's more...

The OpenSSL library provides other hashing algorithms that can be used to generate a hash such as sha and sha1.

See also

The sample code and project for this recipe is located under the MD5 folder in the code bundled with this book.

Escaping a URL

In this recipe, we will learn how to escape URLs using Core Foundation.

Getting ready

In Xcode, create a new Cocoa Application project and name it `Escape`.

How to do it...

1. Click on `EscapeAppDelegate.m` to open it.

2. Add the following code to the `applicationDidFinishLauching:` method:

   ```
   NSString *address = @"http://www.someaddress.com/info?name=Packt
     Publishing";
   address = (NSString
     *)CFURLCreateStringByAddingPercentEscapes(NULL,
     (CFStringRef)address, NULL, (CFStringRef)@"&=? ",
     kCFStringEncodingUTF8);
   NSLog(@"Address: %@", address);
   ```

3. Choose **Build and Run** from the toolbar to run the application.

4. View the console to see the output from running the application.

How it works...

In order to correctly escape characters in a URL, we need to use the Core Foundation function `CFURLCreateStringByAddingPercentEscapes()` and pass in the series of characters we need escaped. Note that `CFStringRef` and `NSString` are bridged so that we can simply cast the `CFStringRef` returned from the `CFURLCreateStringByAddingPercentEscapes()` method to a `NSString` without any issues.

There's more...

The `NSString` class does have a method, `stringByAddingPercentEscapesUsingEncoding:` that can be used, but is limited in the characters it converts to percent escapes.

See also

The sample code and project for this recipe is located under the `Escape` folder in the code bundled with this book.

11
Working with Databases

In this chapter, we will cover:

- ▶ Inserting a row with MySQL
- ▶ Using prepared statements with MySQL
- ▶ Selecting data using MySQL
- ▶ Inserting a row with SQLite
- ▶ Using prepared statements with SQLite
- ▶ Selecting data using SQLite

Introduction

In this chapter, we will explore working with two of the most popular databases used with applications on Mac OS X, MySQL and SQLite. The recipes in this chapter will demonstrate how to connect, insert, and select data using both of these database engines.

 Some recipes in this chapter require you download and install MySQL 5.1. You can download MySQL for Mac OS X at `http://dev.mysql.com/downloads/mysql/5.1.html#downloads`

Inserting a row with MySQL

This recipe will demonstrate how to connect to a MySQL server and insert a row of data into a table.

Getting ready

In Xcode, create a new Cocoa Application project and name it `MySQL Insert`.

Before we can begin executing SQL statements, we need to create a database that we can use when running our recipes. Using the `Terminal.app`, connect to MySQL and create the cocoa database using the following commands:

```
hawk:~ jhawkins$ mysql -u root -p
Enter password:
mysql> create database cocoa;
Query OK, 1 row affected (0.07 sec)
```

How to do it...

1. Click on `MySQL_InsertAppDelegate.m` to open it.

2. Add the import for the mysql.h header file:

   ```
   #import "mysql.h"
   ```

3. Add the following code to the `applicationDidFinishLaunching:` method:

   ```
   NSString *host = @"localhost";
   NSString *user = @"root";
   NSString *password = @"mysql";
   NSString *database = @"cocoa";
   MYSQL *mysql = NULL;

   mysql = mysql_init(mysql);
   if (mysql == NULL) {
     NSLog(@"mysql_init failed. %s", mysql_error(mysql));
     return;
   }

   mysql = mysql_real_connect(mysql, [host UTF8String], [user
     UTF8String], [password UTF8String], [database UTF8String] , 0,
     NULL, 0);
   if (mysql == NULL) {
   ```

```
    NSLog(@"mysql_real_connect failed. %s",mysql_error(mysql));
    return;
}


NSString *sql = @"CREATE TABLE IF NOT EXISTS publishers (id
    INTEGER AUTO_INCREMENT PRIMARY KEY, name VARCHAR(100))";
int result = mysql_query(mysql, [sql UTF8String]);
if (result != 0) {
    NSLog(@"mysql_query failed. %s", mysql_error(mysql));
    mysql_close(mysql);
    return;
}


sql = @"INSERT INTO publishers (id, name) VALUES (NULL, 'Packt
    Publishing')";
result = mysql_query(mysql, [sql UTF8String]);
if (result != 0) {
    NSLog(@"mysql_query failed. %s", mysql_error(mysql));
    mysql_close(mysql);
return;
}


mysql_close(mysql);
```

4. In the Xcode project view, right-click on the **Frameworks** group and choose **Add...**, then choose **Existing Frameworks...**

5. Select **Dylibs** from the popup and then select **libmysqlclient.dylib** from the list:

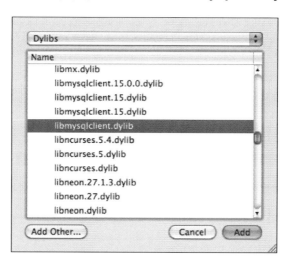

6. From the **Project** menu, choose **Edit Project Settings**.

7. Set the **Header Search Paths** to `/usr/local/mysql/include`.

8. Set the **Library Search Paths** to `/usr/local/mysql/lib`.

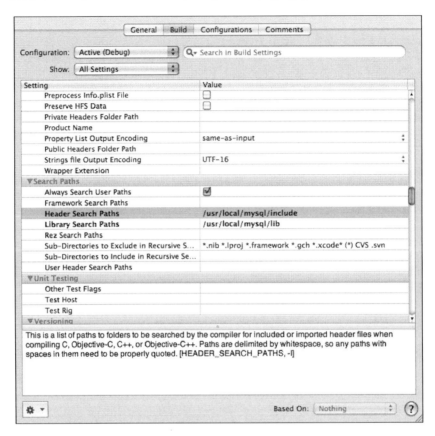

9. Choose **Build and Run** from the toolbar to run the application.

10. Using `Terminal.app`, log in to the MySQL command line client and verify the new row was inserted:

```
hawk:~ jhawkins$ mysql -u root -p
Enter password:
mysql> use cocoa
Database changed
mysql> select * from publishers;
```

```
+----+------------------+
| id | name             |
+----+------------------+
|  1 | Packt Publishing |
+----+------------------+
1 row in set (0.00 sec)
```

How it works...

After adding the MySQL dynamic library to the Xcode project and adding the import for the `mysql.h` header file, we begin by defining a MYSQL data structure that will be used when calling the MySQL API. A call to `mysql_init()` initializes the MYSQL data structure in preparation for calling `mysql_real_connect()`.

When making a connection to the database server, we use the `mysql_real_connect()` method passing the MYSQL data structure, login information, and the host the server is running on. The last parameter is a flag that can be set to a number of different options that specify features for the client connection.

Once connected to the database, we can issue SQL statements using the `mysql_query()` method.

Lastly, we call `mysql_close()` to release the connection to the database server and free the MYSQL data structure.

There's more...

In the example above, we defined our publisher's table as having a column named *id* with a type of INTEGER, and the AUTO_INCREMENT attribute. With the AUTO_INCREMENT attribute defined, we can simply insert a NULL for the *id* column and it will automatically insert the next unique id.

See also

The sample code and project for this recipe is located under the MySQL Insert folder in the code bundled with this book.

Using prepared statements with MySQL

Prepared statements provide a way to safely handle data when working with databases. In this recipe, we will use a prepared statement to bind the publisher's name to the *name* column of our table.

Getting ready

In Xcode, create a new Cocoa Application project and name it MySQL Prepared.

How to do it...

1. Click on MySQL_PreparedAppDelegate.m to open it.

2. Add the import for the mysql.h header file:

   ```
   #import "mysql.h"
   ```

3. Add the following code to the applicationDidFinishLaunching: method:

   ```
   NSString *host = @"localhost";
   NSString *user = @"root";
   NSString *password = @"mysql";
   NSString *database = @"cocoa";
   MYSQL *mysql = NULL;
   MYSQL_STMT *statement = NULL;
   MYSQL_BIND bind[1];

   mysql = mysql_init(mysql);
   if (mysql == NULL) {
     NSLog(@"mysql_init failed. %s", mysql_error(mysql));
     return;
   }

   mysql = mysql_real_connect(mysql, [host UTF8String], [user
     UTF8String], [password UTF8String], [database UTF8String] , 0,
     NULL, 0);
   if (mysql == NULL) {
     NSLog(@"mysql_real_connect failed. %s", mysql_error(mysql));
     return;
   }

   NSString *sql = @"CREATE TABLE IF NOT EXISTS publishers (id
     INTEGER AUTO_INCREMENT PRIMARY KEY, name VARCHAR(100))";
   int result = mysql_query(mysql, [sql UTF8String]);
   if (result != 0) {
     NSLog(@"mysql_query failed. %s", mysql_error(mysql));
     mysql_close(mysql);
     return;
   }

   statement = mysql_stmt_init(mysql);
   ```

```
sql = @"INSERT INTO publishers (id, name) VALUES (NULL, ?)";

result = mysql_stmt_prepare(statement, [sql UTF8String], [sql
  length]);
if (result != 0) {
  NSLog(@"mysql_stmt_prepare failed. %s", mysql_error(mysql));
  mysql_stmt_close(statement);
  mysql_close(mysql);
  return;
}

NSString *parameter = @"Cocoa and Objective-C Cookbook";

char buffer[100] = {'\0'};
my_bool not_null = 0;

strncpy(buffer, [parameter UTF8String], 100);

bzero(bind, sizeof(bind));
bind[0].buffer_type = MYSQL_TYPE_VAR_STRING;
bind[0].buffer = (char *)buffer;
bind[0].buffer_length = strlen(buffer);
bind[0].is_null = &not_null;

my_bool n = mysql_stmt_bind_param(statement, bind);
if (n != 0) {
  NSLog(@"mysql_stmt_bind_param failed. %s", mysql_error(mysql));
  mysql_stmt_close(statement);
  mysql_close(mysql);
  return;
}

result = mysql_stmt_execute(statement);
if (result != 0) {
  NSLog(@"mysql_stmt_execute failed. %s", mysql_error(mysql));
  mysql_stmt_close(statement);
  mysql_close(mysql);
  return;
}

mysql_stmt_close(statement);
mysql_close(mysql);
```

4. In the Xcode project view, right-click on the **Frameworks** group and choose **Add…**, then choose **Existing Frameworks…**

5. Select **Dylibs** from the popup and select **libmysqlclient.dylib** from the list.

6. From the **Project** menu choose **Edit Project Settings**.

7. Set the **Header Search Paths** to `/usr/local/mysql/include`.

8. Set the **Library Search Paths** to `/usr/local/mysql/lib`.

9. Choose **Build and Run** from the toolbar to run the application.

10. Using `Terminal.app` log into the MySQL command line client and verify that the new row was inserted:

```
hawk:~ jhawkins$ mysql -u root -p
Enter password:
mysql> use cocoa
Database changed
mysql> select * from publishers;
+----+--------------------------------+
| id | name                           |
+----+--------------------------------+
| 1  | Cocoa and Objective-C Cookbook |
+----+--------------------------------+
1 row in set (0.00 sec)
```

How it works…

After establishing a connection to the database server and creating our table, if it does not exist, we initialize the `MYSQL_STMT` data structure. The `MYSQL_STMT` structure is used as a handle to all the calls to the MySQL prepared statement methods.

We then call the `mysql_stmt_prepare()` method with the SQL statement for inserting a row into the table. In this case, we are inserting an *id* and *name* into our publisher's table. The *?* character is used as a placeholder for the *name* column within a prepared statement. The placeholder will be substituted when we bind this parameter using the `mysql_stmt_bind_param()` method by passing an array of `MYSQL_BIND` structures, one for each parameter we need to bind in the SQL statement. In our example, we have a single MYSQL_BIND structure since we are binding only the *name* parameter.

The MYSQL_BIND structure needs to have several fields set in order to work correctly. We first set the `buffer_type`, which is set to a constant that represents the same data type used to define the column in the table. Next, we set the buffer to the actual data we want to set into the column. The length of the column's data is set as well. Lastly, we set the `is_null` flag to indicate if we are setting a NULL value for our parameter.

The `mysql_stmt_execute()` method executes the prepared statement with the current bindings. It is important to call the `mysql_stmt_close()` method when finished with the prepared statement in order to free the resources consumed by the use of the prepared statement.

See also

The sample code and project for this recipe is located under the `MySQL Prepared` folder in the code bundled with this book.

Selecting data using MySQL

In this recipe, we will show how to select data from the publisher's table that we have been using through out this chapter.

Getting ready

In Xcode, create a new Cocoa Application project and name it `MySQL Select`.

How to do it...

1. Click on `MySQL_SelectAppDelegate.m` to open it.

2. Add the import for the `mysql.h` header file:

   ```
   #import "mysql.h"
   ```

3. Add the following code to the `applicationDidFinishLaunching:` method:

   ```
   NSString *host = @"localhost";
   NSString *user = @"root";
   NSString *password = @"mysql";
   NSString *database = @"cocoa";
   MYSQL *mysql = NULL;

   mysql = mysql_init(mysql);
   if (mysql == NULL) {
     NSLog(@"mysql_init failed. %s", mysql_error(mysql));
     mysql_close(mysql);
     return;
   }

   mysql = mysql_real_connect(mysql, [host UTF8String], [user
     UTF8String], [password UTF8String], [database UTF8String] , 0,
     NULL, 0);
   ```

```
if (mysql == NULL) {
  NSLog(@"mysql_real_connect failed. %s", mysql_error(mysql));
  mysql_close(mysql);
  return;
}

NSString *sql = @"SELECT * FROM publishers";
int result = mysql_query(mysql, [sql UTF8String]);
if (result != 0) {
  NSLog(@"mysql_query failed. %s", mysql_error(mysql));
    mysql_close(mysql);
  return;
}

MYSQL_RES *mysqlres;
MYSQL_ROW mysqlrow;

mysqlres = mysql_store_result(mysql);
if (mysqlres == NULL) {
  mysql_close(mysql);
  return;
}

mysqlrow = mysql_fetch_row(mysqlres);
while (mysqlrow != NULL) {
  NSLog(@"Name: %s - %s", mysqlrow[0], mysqlrow[1]);
  mysqlrow = mysql_fetch_row(mysqlres);
}

mysql_free_result(mysqlres);
mysql_close(mysql);
```

4. In the Xcode project view, right-click on the **Frameworks** group and choose **Add...**, then choose **Existing Frameworks...**

5. Select **Dylibs** from the popup and then select **libmysqlclient.dylib** from the list.

6. From the **Project** menu, choose **Edit Project Settings**.

7. Set the **Header Search Paths** to /usr/local/mysql/include.

8. Set the **Library Search Paths** to /usr/local/mysql/lib.

9. Choose **Build and Run** from the toolbar to run the application.

10. View the console to see the output from running the application.

How it works...

After connecting to the database server using `mysql_real_connect()` as we have done in the previous recipes, we use the `mysql_query()` method passing the SQL statement to select rows from the database.

To retrieve the row data, we use the `mysql_store_result()` method which returns the resulting row data in a `MYSQL_RES` data structure. To access the individual rows within the `MYSQL_RES` structure, we call the `mysql_fetch_row()` method passing in the `MYSQL_RES` structure. This will return an array of `MYSQL_ROW` data structures, one for each column, containing the column data. You can continue to call `mysql_fetch_row()` until it returns `NULL` to indicate the end of the result set.

In order to free resources after working with the result set, be sure to call the `mysql_free_result()` method.

There's more...

If you need to determine the column types, the MYSQL API provides the `mysql_num_fields()` method which returns an array of `MYSQL_FIELD` data structures, one for each column in the result. The `MYSQL_FIELD` contains the name of the column, its data type, and other information.

See also

The sample code and project for this recipe is located under the `MySQL Select` folder in the code bundled with this book.

Inserting a row with SQLite

Inserting a row into a table with the SQLite C API is fairly simple. This recipe will demonstrate how to insert a single row of data into an SQLite database table.

Getting ready

In Xcode, create a new Cocoa Application project and name it `SQLite Insert`.

How to do it...

1. Click on `SQLite_InsertAppDelegate.m` to open it.

2. Add the import for the sqlite3.h header file:

   ```
   #import "sqlite3.h"
   ```

3. Add the following code to the `applicationDidFinishLaunching:` method:

   ```
   NSString *file = @"/tmp/database.db";
   sqlite3 *database;
   char *errorMessage = NULL;

   int value = sqlite3_open([file UTF8String], &database);
   if (value != SQLITE_OK) {
     NSLog(@"sqlite3_open: %s", sqlite3_errmsg(database));
   }

   NSString *sql = [NSString stringWithFormat:@"CREATE TABLE IF NOT
     EXISTS publishers (id INTEGER, name TEXT)"];

   value = sqlite3_exec(database, [sql UTF8String], NULL, NULL,
     &errorMessage);
   if (value != SQLITE_OK) {
     NSLog(@"sqlite3_exec: %s", errorMessage);
     sqlite3_free(errorMessage);
   }

   sql = [NSString stringWithFormat:@"INSERT INTO publishers (id,
     name) VALUES (1, '%@')", @"Packt Publishing"];

   value = sqlite3_exec(database, [sql UTF8String], NULL, NULL,
     &errorMessage);
   if (value != SQLITE_OK) {
     NSLog(@"sqlite3_exec: %s", errorMessage);
     sqlite3_free(errorMessage);
   }

   sqlite3_close(database);
   ```

4. In the Xcode project view, right-click on the **Frameworks** group and choose **Add...**, then choose **Existing Frameworks...**

5.   Select **Dylibs** from the popup and then select **libsqlite3.dylib** from the list:

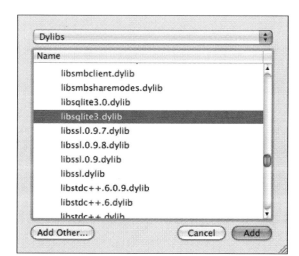

6.   Choose **Build and Run** from the toolbar to run the application.

7.   Using `Terminal.app`, open the `database.db` file using the sqlite3 command line client and verify that the new row was inserted:

```
hawk:tmp jhawkins$ sqlite3 database.db
SQLite version 3.6.12
Enter ".help" for instructions
Enter SQL statements terminated with a ";"
sqlite> select * from publishers;
1|Packt Publishing
```

How it works...

In order to insert data into an SQLite database table, we first need to open the database file. Using the `sqlite3_open()` method, we specify the path to the database file and the pointer to the `sqlite3` data structure.

Once we have opened the database, we can use the `sqlite3_exec()` method to execute our SQL insert statement. In the call to `sqlite3_exec()`, we pass the sqlite3 data structure and the SQL statement. Since we are not executing SQL that returns data, we can set the callback parameter to `NULL`. The last parameter is a character pointer, which will point to an error message if the method fails.

When we are finished with the database, we call `sqlite3_close()` to close the database file and release the sqlite3 data structure.

There's more...

If the `sqlite3_exec()` method returns an error message, use the `sqlite3_free()` method to release memory allocated for the error message.

See also

The sample code and project for this recipe is located under the `SQLite Insert` folder in the code bundled with this book.

Using prepared statements with SQLite

Prepared statements provide you with a way to safely insert or update parameterized data into a table row. This recipe will show you how to use prepared statements with the SQLite database.

Getting ready

In Xcode, create a new Cocoa Application project and name it `SQLite Prepared`.

How to do it...

1. Click on `SQLite_PreparedAppDelegate.m` to open it.

2. Add the import for the sqlite3.h header file:

   ```
   #import "sqlite3.h"
   ```

3. Add the following code to the `applicationDidFinishLaunching:` method:

   ```
   NSString *file = @"/tmp/database.db";
   sqlite3 *database = NULL;
   sqlite3_stmt *statement = NULL;
   char *errorMessage = NULL;

   int value = sqlite3_open([file UTF8String], &database);
   if (value != SQLITE_OK) {
     NSLog(@"sqlite3_open: %s", sqlite3_errmsg(database));
   }

   NSString *sql = [NSString stringWithFormat:@"CREATE TABLE IF NOT
     EXISTS publishers (id INTEGER, name TEXT)"];

   value = sqlite3_exec(database, [sql UTF8String], NULL, NULL,
     &errorMessage);
   ```

```
if (value != SQLITE_OK) {
  NSLog(@"sqlite3_exec: %s", errorMessage);
  sqlite3_free(errorMessage);
}

sql = @"INSERT INTO publishers (id, name) VALUES (1, ?)";

int result = sqlite3_prepare_v2(database, [sql UTF8String], [sql
  length], &statement, NULL);
if (result != SQLITE_OK) {
  NSLog(@"sqlite3_prepare_v2: %s", sqlite3_errmsg(database));
}

NSString *parameter = [NSString stringWithFormat:@"Cocoa and
  Objective-C Cookbook"];
sqlite3_bind_text(statement, 1, [parameter UTF8String], -1,
  SQLITE_TRANSIENT);

result = sqlite3_step(statement);
if(result != SQLITE_DONE) {
  NSLog(@"sqlite3_step: %s", sqlite3_errmsg(database));
} else {
  NSLog(@"last insert row id: %d", sqlite3_last_insert_
rowid(database));
}

result = sqlite3_finalize(statement);
if (result != SQLITE_OK) {
  NSLog(@"sqlite3_finalize: %s", sqlite3_errmsg(database));
}

sqlite3_close(database);
```

4. In the Xcode project view, right-click on the **Frameworks** group and choose **Add...**, then choose **Existing Frameworks...**

5. Select **Dylibs** from the popup and select **libsqlite3.dylib** from the list.

6. Choose **Build and Run** from the toolbar to run the application.

7. Using Terminal.app, open the database.db file using the sqlite3 command line client and verify that the new row was inserted:

```
hawk:tmp jhawkins$ sqlite3 database.db
SQLite version 3.6.12
Enter ".help" for instructions
Enter SQL statements terminated with a ";"
sqlite> select * from publishers;
1|Cocoa and Objective-C Cookbook
```

How it works...

To use prepared statements in an SQLite database, we open the database file using `sqlite3_open()` as we did in the previous recipe.

Once the database is open, we call the `sqlite3_prepare_v2()` method passing in the `sqlite3` data structure returned from the call to open the database file. We also pass the SQL statement using the `?` to mark the parameters we want to bind. We then pass the length of the SQL statement. The next parameter is a pointer to the `sqlite3_stmt` handle, which will be allocated when the method returns. The last parameter is simply `NULL` as we are not interested in knowing the location of the uncompiled SQL statement.

Next, we call the `sqlite3_bind_text()` method to substitute our value for the binded parameter. Note that we use the `SQLITE_TRANSIENT` constant as the last parameter to indicate that the method should make a copy of the SQL statement that we passed as we might change the parameter at some point after the method call.

After binding the parameters, we call the `sqlite3_step()` method to evaluate the prepared statement. The value returned from this method determines what we need to call next to execute the prepared statement successfully. If `SQLITE_DONE` is returned, the method executed without errors. If `SQLITE_BUSY` is returned, the SQLite could not process the request because the database file was locked. If `SQLITE_ERROR` is returned, then you should not try calling the `sqlite3_step()` method again.

When you are finished using the prepared statement, you should call `sqlite3_finalize()` to free the `sqlite3_stmt` data structure.

There's more...

There are several different methods to bind data provided by SQLite depending on the data type being used. Be sure to use the appropriate `sqlite3_bind` method that matches the table column data type to avoid any data conversion issues.

See also

The sample code and project for this recipe is located under the `SQLite Prepared` folder in the code bundled with this book.

Selecting rows using SQLite

When selecting rows using the SQLite C API, it can be difficult to understand how the result data is returned. SQLite uses a `callback` method to efficiently return the result rows. In this recipe, we will select all the columns in our table and print the data to console from the `callback` method so you can see how the `callback` method is invoked for each row of returned data.

Getting ready

In Xcode, create a new Cocoa Application project and name it `SQLite Select`.

How to do it...

1. Click on `SQLite_SelectAppDelegate.m` to open it.

2. Add an import for the `sqlite3.h` header file:

   ```
   #import "sqlite3.h"
   ```

3. Insert the method declaration for the `callback` function below the `@synthesize window;` statement:

   ```
   int callback(void *info, int columns, char **data, char **column);
   ```

4. Add the following code to the `applicationDidFinishLaunching:` method:

   ```
   NSString *file = @"/tmp/database.db";
   sqlite3 *database = NULL;
   char *errorMessage = NULL;

   int value = sqlite3_open([file UTF8String], &database);
   if (value != SQLITE_OK) {
     NSLog(@"sqlite3_open: %s", sqlite3_errmsg(database));
   }

   NSString *sql = [NSString stringWithFormat:@"CREATE TABLE IF NOT
     EXISTS publishers (id INTEGER, name TEXT)"];

   value = sqlite3_exec(database, [sql UTF8String], NULL, NULL,
     &errorMessage);
   if (value != SQLITE_OK) {
     NSLog(@"sqlite3_exec: %s", errorMessage);
     sqlite3_free(errorMessage);
   }
   ```

```
sql = [NSString stringWithFormat:@"INSERT INTO publishers (id,
  name) VALUES (1, 'Packt Publishing')"];

value = sqlite3_exec(database, [sql UTF8String], NULL, NULL,
  &errorMessage);
if (value != SQLITE_OK) {
  NSLog(@"sqlite3_exec: %s", errorMessage);
  sqlite3_free(errorMessage);
}

sql = @"SELECT * FROM publishers";

value = sqlite3_exec(database, [sql UTF8String], callback, NULL,
  &errorMessage);
if (value != SQLITE_OK) {
  NSLog(@"sqlite3_exec: %s", errorMessage);
  sqlite3_free(errorMessage);
}

sqlite3_close(database);
```

5. Next, add the code for the callback method:

```
int callback(void *info, int columns, char **data, char **column)
{

  NSLog(@"Columns: %d", columns);

  for (int i = 0; i < columns; i++) {
    NSLog(@"Column: %s", column[i]);
    NSLog(@"Data: %s", data[i]);
  }

  return SQLITE_OK;
}
```

6. In the Xcode project view, right-click on the **Frameworks** group and choose **Add...**, and then choose **Existing Frameworks...**

7. Select **Dylibs** from the popup and select **libsqlite3.dylib** from the list.

8. Choose **Build and Run** from the toolbar to run the application.

9. View the console to see the output from running the application.

How it works...

In order to select data from SQLite, we use the `sqlite3_exec()` method as we have done in previous recipes. However, we now set a `callback` method in the third parameter. The `callback` method is defined to pass a generic pointer which can be used to pass any type of data to the `callback` method. Also passed to the `callback` are the number of columns, the column data, and the column names of the result set. The `callback` method will be invoked for each row of data returned from the query.

See also

The sample code and project for this recipe is located under the `SQLite Select` folder in the code bundled with this book.

12
Multimedia

In this chapter, we will cover:

- ▸ Playing movies with QuickTime
- ▸ Playing an audio file
- ▸ Using a Core Image filter
- ▸ Getting EXIF information from an image

Introduction

In this chapter, we will work with multimedia such as QuickTime movies and sound. We will also look at using Core Image filters and extracting EXIF metadata from photos.

Playing movies with QuickTime

Using Cocoa's QTKit framework makes playing QuickTime movies within your application fairly simple. In this recipe, we will use the `QTMovieView` to play a movie.

Getting ready

In Xcode, create a new Cocoa Application project and name it `Movie`.

How to do it...

1. Click on `MovieAppDelegate.h` to open it.
2. Add the import for QuickTime:

   ```
   #import <QTKit/QTKit.h>
   ```

3. Right-click on **Frameworks** and choose **Add...**, then choose **Existing Frameworks...**
   Select the **QTKit.framework** and click on **Add**:

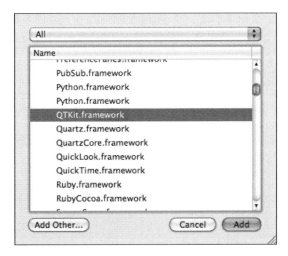

4. Add a variable for the `QTMovieView`:

   ```
   QTMovieView *movieView;
   ```

5. Add a property for the `movieView` variable:

   ```
   @property (assign) IBOutlet QTMovieView *movieView;
   ```

6. Click on the `MovieAppDelegate.m` file to open it.

7. Synthesize the `movieView` variable:

   ```
   @synthesize movieView;
   ```

8. Add the following code to the `applicationDidFinishLaunching:` method:

   ```
   [movieView setControllerVisible:YES];

   NSError *error = nil;
   QTMovie *movie = [QTMovie movieNamed:@"BarrelRace.mov"
     error:&error];
   if (error != nil) {
       [[NSAlert alertWithError:error] runModal];
   }

   [movieView setMovie:movie];
   [[movieView movie] play];
   ```

9. Double-click on **MainMenu.xib** to open the file in Interface Builder.

10. Drag a `QTMovieView` from the **Library** palette to the application window.

11. Right-click on the **Movie App Delegate** to bring up the connections window.

12. Make a connection from the `movieView` outlet to the `QTMovieView` that we dragged to the application window:

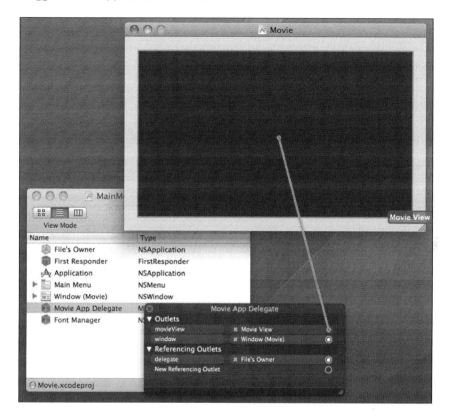

13. Select **Save** from Interface Builder's **File** menu.

14. Back in Xcode, add the `BarrelRace.mov` file from the sample code folder into your project.

15. Choose **Build and Run** from the toolbar to run the application.

How it works...

The `QTMovieView` and `QTMovie` functionality are provided in the QTKit framework. To use these classes you must import the `QTKit.framework` into your Xcode project.

Once we have the Xcode project set up correctly, we can use the `QTMovie` class to load movies by name. We then use the movie view we set up via Interface Builder to set the movie the view will manage. Next, we call the `QTMoive`'s play method to begin playing the movie.

There's more...

The QTMovieView provides many methods to control several aspects of the movie view and the movie itself. You can play, pause, move to the beginning, or move to the end of a movie programmatically. The movie's view can also display a controller to allow users to handle these same actions.

See also

The sample code and project for this recipe is located under the Movie folder in the code bundled with this book.

Playing an audio file

Playing a sound within a Cocoa application is simple using the NSSound class. In this recipe, we will load a sound file from our bundle and play it when the user clicks on our applications Play button.

Getting ready

In Xcode, create a new Cocoa Application project and name it Sound.

How to do it...

1. Click on SoundAppDelegate.h to open the file.

2. Add a property for the button variable:

   ```
   @property (assign) IBOutlet NSButton *button;
   ```

3. Next, add a method declaration for our button action:

   ```
   - (IBAction) buttonHit:(id)sender;
   ```

4. Click on the SoundAppDelegate.m to open it.

5. Synthesize our button variable:

   ```
   @synthesize button;
   ```

6. Add the `buttonHit:` method to the class implementation:

```
- (IBAction) buttonHit:(id)sender {
  NSString *path = [[NSBundle mainBundle] pathForResource:@"p51"
    ofType:@"m4a"];
  NSSound *sound = [[NSSound alloc] initWithContentsOfFile:path
    byReference:NO];
  [sound play];
  [sound release];
}
```

7. Double-click on `MainMenu.xib` to open it in Interface Builder.

8. Drag a **Push Button** from the **Library** palette to the application window.

9. The application window should look similar to the below screenshot:

10. Right-click on the **Sound App Delegate** to open the connections window.

11. Drag a connection from the button outlet to the **Push Button** that we dragged into the application window:

12. Select **Save** from Interface Builder's **File** menu.

13. Back in Xcode, add the `p51.m4a` sound file from the sample code folder into your project.

14. Choose **Build and Run** from the toolbar to run the application.

How it works...

After creating a simple interface for our application consisting of only a play button, we obtain the path of the sound file from our main bundle using `NSBundle`'s `pathForResource: ofType:` method.

Next, we allocate an `NSSound` passing the path of our sound file. To play the sound, we simple call the `play:` method on the returned `NSSound` reference.

There's more...

In some cases, it may be necessary to know when a sound has finished playing. Implementing the `NSSoundDelegate sound:didFinishPlaying` method will notify you when the sound has completed its playback.

See also

The sample code and project for this recipe is located under the `Sound` folder in the code bundled with this book.

Using a Core Image filter

In this recipe, we will use the Core Image Crystallize filter to demonstrate the basics of using a Core Image filter. The filter will apply a crystallizing effect with a large input radius to a sample photo.

Getting ready

In Xcode, create a new Cocoa Application project and name it `Filter`.

How to do it...

1. Click on `FilterAppDelegate.h` to open the file.

2. Add two variables. One for the source image and one for the target image:
   ```
   NSImageView *source;
   NSImageView *target;
   ```

3. Next, add properties for each of the variables:

```
@property (assign) IBOutlet NSImageView *source;
@property (assign) IBOutlet NSImageView *target;
```

4. Click on the `FilterAppDelegate.m` file to open it.

5. Add the import for Quartz header file:

```
#import <QuartzCore/QuartzCore.h>
```

6. Synthesize the source and target variables:

```
@synthesize source;
@synthesize target;
```

7. Add the following code to the `applicationDidFinishLaunching:` method:

```
NSImage *image = [source image];
CIImage *sourceImage = [CIImage imageWithData:[image
  TIFFRepresentation]];

CIFilter *filter = [CIFilter filterWithName:@"CICrystallize"];
[filter setDefaults];
[filter setValue: sourceImage forKey: @"inputImage"];
[filter setValue: [NSNumber numberWithFloat:5.0]
  forKey:@"inputRadius"];

CIImage *filteredImage = [filter valueForKey:@"outputImage"];
image = [[[NSImage alloc] initWithSize:NSMakeSize([filteredImage
  extent].size.width, [filteredImage extent].size.height)]
  autorelease];
[image addRepresentation:[NSCIImageRep
  imageRepWithCIImage:filteredImage]];

[target setImage:image];
```

8. Add the `Photo.jpg` file from the sample code folder into your project.

9. Right-click on **Frameworks** and choose **Add...**, then choose **Existing Frameworks...** Select the **QuartzCore.framework** and click on **Add**.

10. Double-click on `MainMenu.xib` to open it in Interface Builder.

11. Drag two **Custom View**s from the **Library** palette into the application window so that they are side-by-side.

12. Using the **Identity** tab of the Inspector palette, set the **Class** popup of both of the Custom Views to **NSImageView**.

13. Select the left **Custom View**, and then select the **Attributes** tab from the **Inspector** palette. Next, choose `Photo.jpg` from the **Image** popup.

14. When finished, your application window should resemble the screenshot below:

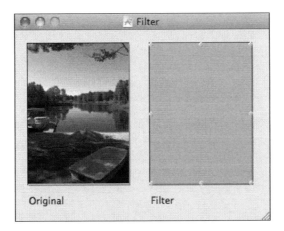

Original   Filter

15. Next, right-click on the **Filter App Delegate** to open the connections window.
16. Drag a connection from the source outlet to the left `NSImageView`.
17. Drag a connection from the target outlet to the right `NSImageView`.
18. Select **Save** from Interface Builder's **File** menu.
19. Back in Xcode, choose **Build and Run** from the toolbar to run the application.

How it works...

We begin by importing the `QuartzCore` framework into your Xcode project and laying out the application window using Interface Builder.

To begin the filtering process, we create a `CIImage` object using the image data from the source image view. We create the `CIFilter` by using the name of the filter; in this case it is the `CICrystallize` filter. By calling the `setDefaults:` method on the `CIFilter`, we initialize the filter with its default values and then only set the properties that we are interested in.

Using the `setValue:forKey:` method, we set various properties of the filter. In our example, we set the `inputImage`, which we created from the source image view. Next, we adjust the value of the `inputRadius` by passing an `NSNumber` with a float value of `5.0`.

Finally, we use the `valueForKey:` method of the filter to get a reference to the filtered image, which we convert, to an `NSImage` so we can set it in the target image view.

You can find more information on the available Core Image filters and their properties at the following link: http://developer.apple.com/library/mac/#documentation/ GraphicsImaging/Reference/CoreImageFilterReference/Reference/ reference.html

See also

The sample code and project for this recipe is located under the `Filter` folder in the code bundled with this book.

Getting EXIF information from an image

In this recipe, we will access a few of the EXIF metadata properties of a photo. The EXIF metadata contains many of the device settings used when the photo was taken such as the shutter speed, focal length, and the date.

Getting ready

In Xcode, create a new Cocoa Application project and name it `EXIF`.

How to do it...

1. Click on the `FilterAppDelegate.m` file to open it.

2. Add the following code to the `applicationDidFinishLaunching:` method:

```
NSString *path = [[NSBundle mainBundle] pathForResource:@"Photo"
  ofType:@"jpg"];

NSBitmapImageRep *bitmapImageRep = [NSBitmapImageRep
  imageRepWithContentsOfFile:path];
if (bitmapImageRep != nil) {
  NSDictionary *exifDictionary = [bitmapImageRep
    valueForProperty:@"NSImageEXIFData"];
  if (exifDictionary != nil) {
    NSNumber *exposureTime = [exifDictionary
      valueForKey:@"ExposureTime"];
    if (exposureTime != nil) {
      NSDecimalNumber *shutterSpeed = [[NSDecimalNumber one]
        decimalNumberByDividingBy: [NSDecimalNumber
        decimalNumberWithString:[exposureTime stringValue]]];
```

```
NSNumberFormatter *numberFormatter = [[[NSNumberFormatter
    alloc] init] autorelease];
[numberFormatter setFormat:@"###0"];
NSLog(@"Exposure: 1/%@", [numberFormatter
    stringFromNumber:shutterSpeed]);
}

NSNumber *fnumber = [exifDictionary
    valueForKey:@"FNumber"];
if (fnumber != nil) {
    NSLog(@"f/%@", [fnumber stringValue]);
}

NSArray *isoSpeed = [exifDictionary
    valueForKey:@"ISOSpeedRatings"];
if (isoSpeed != nil && [isoSpeed count] > 0) {
    NSNumber *speed = [isoSpeed objectAtIndex:0];
    NSLog(@"ISO %@", [speed stringValue]);
}

NSString *dateTime = [exifDictionary
    valueForKey:@"DateTimeOriginal"];
if (dateTime != nil) {
    NSLog(@"Date: %@", dateTime);
}

NSNumber *focalLength = [exifDictionary
    valueForKey:@"FocalLength"];
if (focalLength != nil) {
    NSLog(@"Focal Length: %@", [focalLength stringValue]);
}
    }
}
```

3. Add the Photo.jpg file from the sample code folder into your project.

4. Choose **Build and Run** from the toolbar to run the application.

5. View the console to see the output from running the application.

How it works...

We begin by retrieving the images path from our applications main bundle. Next, we create an `NSBitmapImageRep` with the contents of our image file. Now that we have the reference to the bitmap image, we can use the `valueForProperty:` method by passing the property `NSImageEXIFData` to retrieve an `NSDictionary` of EXIF values. Once you have the dictionary of EXIF values, you can use the keys defined in Apple's CGImageProperties Reference documentation to retrieve the values. In our simple recipe, we get the shutter speed, fnumber, iso speed, date, time and the focal length.

There's more...

Since the EXIF information is returned in an `NSDictionary`, you can enumerate the keys of the dictionary to see what properties are available.

You can also find information on EXIF properties at the following location: `http://developer.apple.com/library/mac/#documentation/GraphicsImaging/Reference/CGImageProperties_Reference/Reference/reference.html`

See also

The sample code and project for this recipe is located under the `EXIF` folder in the code bundled with this book.

Index

[PACKT] Thank you for buying
PUBLISHING **Cocoa and Objective-C Cookbook**

About Packt Publishing

Packt, pronounced 'packed', published its first book "*Mastering phpMyAdmin for Effective MySQL Management*" in April 2004 and subsequently continued to specialize in publishing highly focused books on specific technologies and solutions.

Our books and publications share the experiences of your fellow IT professionals in adapting and customizing today's systems, applications, and frameworks. Our solution based books give you the knowledge and power to customize the software and technologies you're using to get the job done. Packt books are more specific and less general than the IT books you have seen in the past. Our unique business model allows us to bring you more focused information, giving you more of what you need to know, and less of what you don't.

Packt is a modern, yet unique publishing company, which focuses on producing quality, cutting-edge books for communities of developers, administrators, and newbies alike. For more information, please visit our website: www.packtpub.com.

Writing for Packt

We welcome all inquiries from people who are interested in authoring. Book proposals should be sent to author@packtpub.com. If your book idea is still at an early stage and you would like to discuss it first before writing a formal book proposal, contact us; one of our commissioning editors will get in touch with you.

We're not just looking for published authors; if you have strong technical skills but no writing experience, our experienced editors can help you develop a writing career, or simply get some additional reward for your expertise.

Cocos2d for iPhone 0.99 Beginner's Guide

ISBN: 978-1-849513-16-6   Paperback: 368 pages

Make mind-blowing 2D games for iPhone with this fast, flexible, and easy-to-use framework!

1. A cool guide to learning cocos2d with iPhone to get you into the iPhone game industry quickly

2. Learn all the aspects of cocos2d while building three different games

3. Add a lot of trendy features such as particles and tilemaps to your games to captivate your players

Core Data iOS Essentials

ISBN: 978-1-849690-94-2   Paperback: 340 pages

A fast-paced, example-driven guide guide to data-drive iPhone, iPad, and iPod Touch applications

1. Covers the essential skills you need for working with Core Data in your applications

2. Particularly focused on developing fast, light weight data-driven iOS applications

3. Builds a complete example application. Every technique is shown in context

4. Completely practical with clear, step-by-step instructions

Please check **www.PacktPub.com** for information on our titles

MySQL Admin Cookbook

ISBN: 978-1-847197-96-2   Paperback: 376 pages

99 great recipes for mastering MySQL configuration and administration

1. Set up MySQL to perform administrative tasks such as efficiently managing data and database schema, improving the performance of MySQL servers, and managing user credentials

2. Deal with typical performance bottlenecks and lock-contention problems

3. Restrict access sensibly and regain access to your database in case of loss of administrative user credentials

CryENGINE 3 Cookbook

ISBN: 978-1-849691-06-2   Paperback: 424 pages

Over 100 recipes written by Crytek developers for creating AAA games using the technology that created Crysis 2

1. Begin developing your AAA game or simulation by harnessing the power of the award winning CryENGINE3

2. Create entire game worlds using the powerful CryENGINE 3 Sandbox

3. Create your very own customized content for use within the CryENGINE3 with the multiple creation recipes in this book

Please check **www.PacktPub.com** for information on our titles

Made in the USA
Lexington, KY
15 August 2011